Thirty Years of Mondays

Dare to Care: A Guide for New Teachers

Jeff McMillan

1st WORLD PUBLISHING

Thirty Years of Mondays

Dare to Care: A Guide for New Teachers

Jeff McMillan

© Jeff McMillan 2010

Published by 1stWorld Publishing
P.O. Box 2211, Fairfield, Iowa 52556
tel: 641-209-5000 • fax: 866-440-5234
web: www.1stworldpublishing.com

First Edition

LCCN: 2009943671
SoftCover ISBN: 978-1-4218-9139-2
HardCover ISBN: 978-1-4218-9140-8
eBook ISBN: 978-1-4218-9141-5

To my high school teacher Hugh, who taught me the power of caring.

To Anne, who helped me climb higher than I ever imagined possible.

To those teachers I worked with over thirty years, who taught me that teaching was all about giving and sharing.

To all the students I have taught, who gave me the courage to be a better person.

Table of Contents

Introduction

For thirty years I was a story teller. My students were a captivated audience, often subjected to my warped sense of humour and the subjects of my joy for teaching and life. I never missed an opportunity to bring laughter into my lessons or to relate an experience from my childhood. The students would sit in anticipation as they could see the spark in my eyes when they knew a story was on the horizon. The students would work endlessly for the reward of me telling about my first kiss in elementary school and how I was coached by a more "experienced couple" on the other side of the tree. To them I was more than a teacher, I was a real person with experiences just like them. I loved to hear them laugh as I would recant the trials and tribulations of growing up in the sixties, of tales of being the oldest in the family and of the horrors of sharing a bedroom with my brother. Although there are many stories that I would never share with my students, I never missed the chance to display my love for life and the joy of growing up. Imagine me, a fifty-five year old man, telling a group of early teens about my first "date" and how my entire allowance of fifty cents was spent on a large coke for my companion while I drank a free glass of water and them sitting, listening to my every word.

Never would a day pass that I was not asked to tell them a story. I must admit that I used the "story" to my advantage and it was not an everyday occurrence. Several days might pass and the day would be void of any story, however the room was never empty of laughter. Students love it when you "play" with them.

Each student can be played with in his or her special way. They all want the attention of the teacher. Some enjoy being teased in front of the class while others love the private joke. The key is to know when to use levity and how to successfully bring the students back to task. You want the students excited but not out of control. You want them relaxed and comfortable and eager to be there.

One story that I have told over my thirty years of teaching has become part of my legacy. The initial story has grown into an urban legend and became so much more powerful that I could have ever imagined. I have always kept the ending a mystery. There has never been a class that has been told how the story ended. Throughout my career I have met many of my former students and to this day they all ask the same question,"How did you get that girl out of your father's car?"

The story began when I was in grade twelve. I was a fairly popular student. I played on the football and basketball teams and I was dating one of the prettiest girls in the school. I usually played up the "pretty girl" stuff for my students as I would listen to their collective groans. During this time in high school it became apparent to me that I had drawn the attention of a grade niner. At first I didn't notice that she was always in places I was. After a short time it became obvious to me and my friends that she was "stalking" me. Stalking was a great word because it created a ton of mental images for the students and added to the excitement of the story. Everywhere I went, there she was, staring in silence with this strange look on her face. The students loved this as I had them visualize the stare. My friends were going wild with anticipation. I was getting more and more concerned. I had not told my girlfriend about this because I didn't know how to tell her so I kept it a secret.

At that time I had a part-time job working at a grocery store. One Friday night I asked my Dad if I could take the car to work as I wanted to go to my girlfriend's house when I was finished. My work was over at nine thirty and as I was leaving the store I noticed that someone was sitting in the passenger seat of my father's car. My mind was racing. Who could this be? How did they get in the car? What are they doing? What do they want? As I got closer I discovered to my horror that it was my stalker. I was living my greatest nightmare. I opened the car door and asked her what she was doing. She said nothing as she stared deep into my eyes with that "look." I asked her politely to leave. She said nothing as she continued to stare at me. I told her I needed her out of the car as I was going to meet my girlfriend. She said nothing as she continued her stare in silence. I was beginning to panic. I didn't know how I was going to get her out of my car. My mind was racing and my heart was beating faster and faster.

This is where my story ends. The students always went out of their minds with anticipation as they begged for me to finish the story. I never did tell the end of the story. The truth is the ending is anti-climactic. I could never tell them an ending that would be better than the one created in their imaginations.

Over time, this story was passed on from brother to sister, from student to student and even parents. Every class waited for the telling of the story and hoped that they would be the class privileged enough to hear the ending. I have to admit that every year the story got better. Imagine students I taught thirty years ago asking me how I got the girl out of my car.

I am a deeply passionate person and I wear my feelings close to the surface. My students usually knew how deeply I felt about things. Occasionally when speaking of something close to my heart they would see tears in my eyes. They could sense my joy and love for them. They knew how deeply I believed in them because they could see it on my face and hear it in my words. They knew the depths of my disappointments because I openly talked about how I felt. They knew my support for them was unquestionable and that regardless of what happened today, tomorrow was a new day to begin again.

I was very professional in the way I worked with my students and how I addressed issues. Despite my desire for the students to see me as a real person, I was also aware of my responsibilities as a teacher. I always knew where the line was and I would never cross it. You must remain the adult in the room. You must set an example and display appropriate behaviour. You are a model to them. Being close to your students is critical in creating a positive learning environment, but being too close is dangerous. The key is to make each one of them feel special in a way that is acceptable and appropriate. Be there for them, laugh with them, show them you care, let them know that you are there to guide them towards becoming better at what they do and to help them take a step towards their dreams.

I loved teaching right up to the last bell. I cannot recall a single day that I was not excited to go to school. It was such a pleasure to work with young people. They are curious and full of energy. Their lives are unfolding in front of us and they look to us for guidance. The influence we have can never be underestimated. If done correctly, the results of good teaching will be with them for the rest of their lives.

There were many tears around the school when I decided to retire. Students would come up to me and beg me to stay. I was very flattered and touched by their comments. It was a difficult decision but one that was right for me. To help the students understand I came up with a plan to illustrate my years in education and why the time had come for me to move on. During my last assembly I had a young boy in kindergarten come and stand beside me as I delivered my final message to the students. With my arm around this young four year old, I told the students to take a good look at him for what they were seeing was me, fifty years ago. I began school as a young, innocent, energetic, little boy and here I was today a fifty-five year old man. I had been going to school for over fifty years. I could tell by the look in their eyes that they understood. I had given almost my entire life to education and it was time to do something else. We all cried together as I waved a final good-bye.

What I plan to share with you in this book comes from years of experience and from being "new" in different schools. I began, like most of you, eager to do well and armed with no experience. I made my mistakes, but thankfully, I was surrounded by excellent, experienced teachers who guided and helped me gain the confidence and skills required to be a successful teacher. Always learn from those more experienced. They were you once.

Teaching is the most wonderful profession on this planet. We get a chance to touch the lives of those we work with. We help make the world a better place and we give young minds the opportunity to grow. None of this happens without hard work and dedication. There is nothing easy about teaching. You have to be prepared and ready for every day. The challenges you will face are deep and everlasting. Like the students you work with, you must have a desire to learn and a thirst for knowledge. Care enough to take teaching seriously. Care enough to stay current. Care enough to meet the individual needs of each student. Care enough to provide your students with a challenging program that will engage them in their learning. Care enough to be there for them and care enough to get them the help they need. Just care enough and all will be well.

Chapter One
Setting Up Your Class For Success

Setting Up Your Class / Managing Physical Space

One of the greatest memories in a teacher's career is that moment when you enter your class for the first time. You find your eyes moving quickly around the room and your mind races as you begin to think of the possibilities. You have completed your formal training as a teacher, practice rounds have been a success.

The thought now strikes you... this class is mine, all mine. Now what do I do?

The room has been cleaned by the custodians during the summer. The floors shine, the walls are clean, the desks stand in rows and the walls and bulletin boards are empty. A flash enters your mind of the way rooms looked when you were a student, and over time, how the classroom structure has changed. You think about your student teacher experiences and what you liked and disliked about their class setup. The time has arrived and you are going to give this room your personal touch. You are going to set up this class to meet your needs. Question is, do you make it pretty or do you make it functional? Your classroom has to be both teacher- and student-friendly.

Creating Freedom of Movement

The first consideration is how to make this room work for you and allow your students the ability to work freely. You need to be able to manage the space effectively and efficiently. Not all rooms are the same size and shape; however, the need for both your movement and the movement of the students is critical. Your ability to easily access your students is very important. Students need to be aware that you can quickly get to them if they have a question or if they are experiencing a problem.

Many behaviour situations can be avoided when the students know you are freely "working the crowd," or that you may teach from their part of the room. Seldom should you find yourself teaching from the front of the room.

The days of the Sage on the Stage and the old Socratic method of delivering information is long gone. We now have our students engaged in partnership activities, cooperative learning experiences and team work. Discussion and sharing information with team members and classmates is critical and, therefore, consideration must be made to allow for this type of student engagement.

Setting up your class so that students can work as effective groups requires careful planning and a good understanding of the type of students you will have working together, their skill levels and their learning styles. Not all students are ready to work as effective team members. Such skills must be taught and practised on an ongoing basis. Therefore, it is important that you have a discussion with other teachers who have worked with these students before you set up your classroom.

Your goal is to create a positive and successful learning environment for everyone, including yourself. Gather as much information as you can about the "nature of the beast" before you start moving the desks.

Like adults, working in groups often encourages discussion and often this discussion can be off-topic. If you want to see how ineffective groups can be, you only need to look as far as your own colleagues during professional activity days. Seldom will you find all teachers on task and often you will see them engaged in topics far beyond what is being discussed. The difference, however, is that most teachers can pull themselves together to finish the task at hand. Not all students are capable of this feat, due largely to their lack of team skills. Don't be surprised that your students don't work effectively in these groups you have designed. Remember, group work requires that you to teach the skills and provide them with the opportunity to practise these skills.

The days of a teacher standing in front of the class and lecturing while the students repeat or take notes is long over. Today a number of new techniques have replaced the outdated Socratic method of imparting knowledge. Good teachers use a variety of teaching methods to address the specific needs of their students. Often these strategies and techniques will involve the use a variety of strategically selected groupings. The effectiveness of the group will ultimately lead to the depth of understanding and learning. Understanding how to use different types of groupings is very important. Effective grouping strategies can help students develop skills in teamwork, communication, human relations and social interaction as well as promoting self-confidence, values and morals and improving higher order thinking skills. Among the many activities that can contribute to the development of these skills are cooperative learning strategies, which are very effective. Cooperative learning relies on the positive interdependence of team members working together towards a common goal. These strategies can be very simple and applied at almost anytime. They can also be very complex, requiring in-depth planning and preparation.

Class Setup and Routines

The establishment of effective routines in your class is one of the first skills you want to introduce to your students. Routines such as entering the class in the morning or after a break, subject transition, movement in the class, movement out of the class, answering questions, passing in assignments, gathering supplies, money collection, eating lunch, indoor breaks during inclement weather and dismissal all require a class setup whereby movement is easy and controlled. Remember, if you don't control your class, the students will be more than glad to do this for you. Someone is going to be in charge. It is best that it be you.

Classroom Setup and the Custodian (Health and Safety)

In all fairness to our custodial staff, they have a job of cleaning up after us upon completion of our day. They would prefer that the class is set up so that they can clean easily and quickly. Obstacles and weird groupings often make their job difficult. What is best for you and your students is the main concern. Teaching is not about making life easy for others, but it is important to be reasonable. Schools are a place of learning. Although we must try to be onside with our custodians, we cannot allow their priorities to dominate. If a problem does arise seek clarification from your principal. They can be great mediators in these situations.

Creating a warm and inviting environment requires some understanding of the significance of colours and the effects colours can have in a learning environment. We cannot always control the colour of our walls. That is a decision made by the maintenance staff in your board and although we may often want to question their thinking, there is very little we can do with the base colour. We do, however, have control over the colours we use in other parts of our room. Ideally we want our class to be warm, calm and orderly. Colours such as blues and greens tend to calm, relax and nurture our students. The use of negative, blank space and the use of light neutral colours can also foster calmness. If our goal is to increase student participation, involvement, engagement, interest and to help them focus on the subject then being careful not to over-stimulate is something to consider. It is also important to realize that the number of students in our class that experience symptoms of ADD, ADHD, Autism, Asbergers and other learning difficulties are on the rise, and these students can be easily overstimulated by colour as well as other distracting factors.

What should be on the walls of your class should be of educational value and enhance the learning process. Your walls should be a reference point for the students, a place they can find an answer, see a connection, observe an example, find a direction, see a model of quality. Any information placed on the walls should be readable from the student's vantage point.

But I'm A Guy!!!!

It is important for you to understand from the outset that I am a "guy." Although this is a huge generalization, often there is a difference between how a male teacher and a female teacher prepares his/her classroom. The difference can also be seen as we compare primary, junior and intermediate teachers. It is not uncommon to see beginning male teachers having their mothers, sisters, girlfriends or anyone else assist them with getting their room ready for the new year. I myself have used the "but I'm a guy" excuse for years and although it has gotten many laughs, the truth is my class was not always aesthetically pleasing to the students as they arrived the first day. Your classroom is a world of learning, a place for creativity and challenges. It is an environment that your students will be in for the next two hundred days. You and they want to feel comfortable and yet stimulated within these walls. Be careful not to under-stimulate or over-stimulate your students. Provide guides for learning, cues for what to do next, examples, anchor charts and exemplars of what you are looking for, rubrics for guidance, anything that is going to help the student become a better performer and assist them when taking chances and working independently. Examples of their good work is great; however, I am always reluctant to do so because of the effect it can often have on the struggling student. Be wise and display everyone's work if that is something you see as beneficial to your students.

Avoid using "wallpaper" or commercial, teacher-made materials. Although your room may appear "pretty," if what is on the walls has no relation to what is being taught then it is redundant. I used to cover my walls with purchased posters of witty sports sayings. I thought it looked cool but I know I never really referenced any of the messages throughout the year. I was simply trying to fill up space with unrelated material. It took me a while to realize that my classroom was a place of learning and not an art gallery. The walls of your classroom should be filled with quality look-fors that can be used by the students to enhance learning.

Quality Educational Look-Fors

✎ Anchor Charts

✎ Word Walls / Vocabulary Charts

✎ Rubrics / Assignment Checklists

✎ Student Generated Bulletin Boards

- ✍ Flow Charts
- ✍ Links with the Curriculum
- ✍ Current writing samples
- ✍ Good quality student art

Learning happens everywhere !!!!!!!!!!

All teachers are so proud when they first enter their new class and they sit down in the "teacher's desk," usually located somewhere at the front of the room. It is a symbol of our rites of passage. We are no longer confined to a student's desk and we have graduated to the position of "Leader of the Class." If we look back on teaching over the last many years, we can usually recall the teacher's desk as being a central fixture in the room. This is the place where you hand in assignments, where the teacher calls you to discuss work and work-related problems. This is where you are asked to sit near when you have a problem focusing your attention. This desk symbolizes the centre of learning. Ask any student, even today, if they want to work at your desk and watch their response. Some teachers have made their desk a shrine yet it should not be the focus of learning.

I suggest you either get rid of that desk or locate it somewhere out of the way. It is big, cumbersome and takes up way too much space.

Seldom will you ever see good teachers sitting at their desks. I have seen some over the years actually teach from their desks. I was told once that teachers that do this are in semi-retirement mode. Think about the message that is being sent when you can't even stand to deliver a lesson or that if they need help they must raise their hand and come to you. Get that desk out of the way. Create movement for you and your students.

How the environment in our class affects student learning is something that every teacher must consider. If teachers are magnetic and can hold a student's attention through engagement and passion, if they can provide students with meaningful real world learning experiences, then they could teach in a darkened mud puddle in the basement and have a profound effect. If teachers are a total bore, confusing, poorly prepared, unskilled, have no ability to draw the student in to their learning, even a stunning, fabulous, well-organized, colourful room will do little to affect student learning and engagement.

Chapter Two
The First Minute / The First Day / The First Week

I can still remember the feelings that I had the night before I started my first teaching job. I was fresh out of teacher's college. I had been in early and chatted with the teachers I was working with in my division. I had been told the history of some of my students. I had carefully planned out how I wanted my room to look. I was ready to teach yet sleep was hard to come by. To say I was nervous would have been a gross understatement. This was now my room and these were my kids and what they were going to do was all up to me. I had completed my teacher education and I had worked with excellent teachers in my teaching rounds but now these students were all mine. I was the one in control.

I arrived at school early the first day, checked the room over, wrote my name and the date on the board. I made sure the students had notebooks, pencils, rulers and erasers. Ten minutes before the bell, I sat down at my desk that was strategically located at the back of the room and then I had this terrible thought go through my head....what do I do now? The bell rang and it was show time. In they came, each of them staring at me like I had four heads. I was new, young, inexperienced and they knew it. They were curious to know what I was all about. The advantage that an experienced teacher has over a new teacher is that they have a history, a

legacy, so to speak, and with that comes anticipated expectations from the students. Being new, I had no established rep-
utation. I was ripe for the picking, I knew that and so did
they.

The First Minute

Your classroom is a place where students come to learn. You
are the person who is responsible for those students. You, as the
teacher, are the adult in charge. You are in control. What you do
in the first thirty seconds to a minute will determine in a student's mind who will run this class. If they see you as organized,
prepared, consistent and fair, then you have established yourself
as the leader. If they feel that you are flying by the seat of your
pants and that when you say "no" it probably means "maybe"
or if you let behaviour issues go, then they see themselves as in
control. The way you deal with each student and what you have
them do upon entry on the first day is so important to your
credibility. Credibility is what you want. It is what you must
establish, and, believe it or not, the students are hoping that
you are the person in charge. Students love a teacher that knows
what they are doing. Students want their teachers to lead.

On day one, the first thing a teacher needs to do in order to
establish who is in control of the class, is to assign seating. After
talking with last years' teachers you should know who should not
be sitting beside each other. The advantage of you establishing
the seating arrangement is that you are telling the students that
what happens in the class is directed by you. I have seen teachers
who allow students to enter the class on the first day and pick
their own seats. Ultimately, what happens is that friends sit with
friends, behaviour issues sit with behaviour issues, students push

and fight for "best seats" (usually far away from the front and the teacher's desk), and the room within the first minute is filled with chaos. Unhappy students often let their feelings be known and the rest of the class is watching to see how you are going to bring this confusion under control. By having the students find a desk with their name on it, you are avoiding this confusion and creating calm immediately. Remember, you also have a master seating plan. You know them before they know you.

Once the students have found their seats, it is also important that you have them begin to work on something—after all, school is a place where students come to work.

What better thing to do on the first day and in the first few minutes than to establish the philosophy that when you come to my class we are here to work.

I have the students complete an information card concerning their address, phone numbers, parents' names, brothers and sisters and so on. I use these information cards throughout the year when making calls and setting up interview times. The other tasks I want the students to complete are written on the board. I am establishing my credibility from the beginning.

Name: Parent's Names: (Often Different)	Date of Birth:
Home Address:	Phone Numbers:
Parent's Work:	Work Numbers:
Siblings:	Hobbies/Interests:
Out of School Jobs:	

The First Challenge

How you deal with your first challenge is very important to establishing your credibility. Dealing with behaviour comes before instruction and teaching. There is an old myth that is passed on to new teachers, that is, "You can't smile until Christmas." That is the most ridiculous statement ever made, however, it is important to establish the first day that you are a kind and caring person but you will not tolerate poor behaviour in your class. Bad behaviour is disruptive and prevents others from learning. It is your job to deal with it and prevent it from re-occurring.

Gaining control of a class is not as difficult as it appears; however, trying to get control after you have lost it is a very difficult task filled with pain and sorrow.

Once you have established yourself as a pushover, it is very hard to change that impression. Meet the first challenge head on. Stop what you are doing. Be firm, be fair and be consistent. Try to keep it as low key as you can while still making your point. Don't become a screamer. It won't be long until all the students tune you out. The tone of your voice is important. You want your students to recognize differences in your voice and what those differences mean. Everyone needs to know that you will deal with behaviour. Being liked and being respected can be two very different objectives in teaching. Many new teachers want desperately to be liked and as a result they often overlook behaviour as a way of avoiding confrontation. The difficulty here lies in the assumption that if a student likes you as a person, they will work hard for you as a teacher. That simply is not the case. Respect is the critical part of the behaviour equation. Yes, we must be kind and caring but we do not need to be their friends. We are their teachers and we are the adults.

Standing in front of a group of students can be a humbling experience for most new teachers. What becomes painfully obvious is the fact that the students watch and study our every move. They check out the clothing we wear, the way we comb our hair, the way we walk, the tone of our voice, the way we phrase things and so on. During my first day as a teacher, I became aware of two important pieces of personal information. The first, as the students pointed out to me, was the fact that my writing on the board was difficult for them to read. After years of university note taking and scribbles, I had developed very poor handwriting skills. I could make an excuse by saying that writing with chalk was not an easy task but the truth was that I had just become lazy. The second important piece of information came from the laughter throughout the room as I began to write on the chalkboard. When I asked what everyone found so funny a little girl in the front row raised her hand and said, " Your bum wiggles when you write." I knew I had some work to do on myself. From that moment on I worked hard to improve my handwriting and when I did put something on the board I consciously squeezed my butt cheeks together as I knew the eyes of the world were watching.

Establishing Rules and Routines - Practice Makes Perfect

Rules and procedures are only valuable when all partners buy into them. Many teachers begin the first day with a long list of rules they have deemed important. It should be no shock that the students don't always view these rules with the same importance. Often teachers will outline the various class rules and the consequences for failure to comply. Although this may appear on the surface as the teachers establishing authority, in reality it is nothing short of declaring themselves to be dictators and like many dictators there is usually a group plotting to overthrow them.

The establishment of class rules and routines is a joint effort between the teacher and the students.

The teacher must create a need for such procedures and have the class, as a team, address ways of meeting that need. When your students become part of the solution to a problem, they then take on ownership of the situation and often become advocates for the cause.

Rules are not new to students. As they move from grade to grade, they are constantly aware that being in school has certain expectations on them. They are aware that teachers are responsible for what happens in the class and that there is a need to eliminate the possibility of chaos throughout the day. They know that there are bigger rules beyond the classroom that also dictate how they must behave. All students, after a very short time in school, are aware that there are consequences for inappropriate behaviour. The establishment of rules is nothing new to students.

The successful implementation of class rules and procedures depends greatly on how you introduce them, how much the students buy into them and how consistently you follow through. A rule and procedure is of no value if you have no intention of making it work on a day-to-day basis.

As a teacher, you are the master manipulator. You know in your own mind exactly how you want your class to operate. Your mission is to establish those conditions by making the students think that they are equal partners in the creation of the class procedures. Brainstorming and team-building activities are very useful when establishing the need for class rules. The establishment of a collective contract, or a set of rules developed and agreed on by the class, can be successfully created using many cooperative learning strategies. Out of this process comes the beginning of a sense of team. You want your students to see themselves as a group, all working together for the good of the entire class. You want all of them to buy in to your master plan.

Building a Sense of Team

The first day of class is a time for you to get to know your students and a time for them to get to know you. Students want to know that you are real and that you have a life beyond teaching. Early on the first day, you will want to have the students engage in an activity that gets them talking about who they are, their interests, their likes and dislikes. This is important on many levels. First, it establishes the beginning of trust in your room. Students are telling you about themselves. They will be watching you very closely to see how you react to them as individuals. Secondly, it is the beginning of you creating a class identity, a sense of team. It is important that your students view themselves as unique individuals. The students want to believe that they are valued for their individuality and yet also valued as a group of people who will share similar experiences for the next two hundred school days.

Creating a sense of team is not an easy task. It requires careful planning and the effective teaching of the skills required by all team members. Don't expect, that on the first day, your idea of a team will come together. Many students have never been taught how to be an effective team member. Many are not aware of how to actively listen or how to disagree in an agreeable way. Often, students are expected to be on the team with no knowledge of what that means. Your job, throughout the year, is to give students those experiences and the opportunity to practise. Anything is possible once your class begins to operate as a unit, as an effective team with a shared and common goal.

TEAM BUILDING SKILLS

Team Environment - Positive Interaction and Praise

Team Effectiveness - Active Listening Skills

Conflict and Criticism - Disagreeing in an Agreeable Way

Team Problem Solving Skills - Focus

Persuasion Strategies - Presenting an Argument

Quality Control / Setting Your Standard

The best work you will ever receive from a student is defined by the worst work you will accept.

The establishment of your standard of "good work" has to be done very early on the first day or during the first week. Many students will be very happy to give you a minimal effort on most assignments unless you make it very clear that you will not accept anything less than their best effort. The ideal goal for you as a teacher is to get your students to always give a good effort in everything they do.

It is important for your students to feel comfortable around you. They need to see you as someone who is there to help them get better. Not all students are going to reach the top of the mountain at the same time. With careful planning, effective feed-back and good mentoring, all students can move towards the peak. We must assist every student on their journey and make sure that with each step they make we are there to help them become stronger. They need to know that reaching the top can only be achieved by giving a strong effort in everything they do. Your role is to see that they always give that best effort.

I tell my students very early in the year that I don't want them to work hard for me or their parents. I want them to work hard for themselves and to be proud of what they do and what they accomplish. I want them to submit work to me because they are confident that what they have done is a reflection of the hard work they put into that assignment. I want them to see my feedback as a way of making themselves better as learners. They need to see themselves as the centre and main player in their learning and they need to have the opportunity to show others just how great they can be. This is best accomplished in front of a real audience.

Asking a student to redo or rethink an assignment is not such a bad thing. How you give your feedback will determine how the student will view themselves as a learner. Harsh words such as, "This is unacceptable," or in some cases such archaic practices as destroying a student's work can lead to resentment and a refusal to move forward. Your words can be like poison and your feedback can fall on deaf ears, especially if the student sees you as judge and executioner.

Uncaring criticism does nothing to help the student do better.

You want the students to improve their performance, thus giving them the strength and courage to take the next step. You need to give them the skills and encouragement to give their best effort, not because you want them to but because they want to. Your assessment of their work needs to be positive and productive. They need to know what is required to make it better. They just need your help and advice to get there.

Teachers are infamous for finding the one mistake in a long essay. I, myself, have given long workshops, only to be interrupted by a teacher that has found a small error on one of my power point slides. Finding the error is easy. Rubbing a student's face in the mistake often prevents the student from moving in a forward direction. I am not saying the error should not be addressed but how it is pointed out is critical. The key is to find the steps that have been done correctly up to the error and then discuss what the next step should be. "You have a good understanding of what is happening to this point, the next thing I would like you to do is look at example three on the board."

My daughter and I had many conversations during her years in high school. Often she spoke of the positive influences her teachers had on her education. Occasionally, she would discuss the disappointments she had experienced with teachers who were less than caring. She would express her feelings of anger when a teacher would humiliate the class by flicking the lights on and off and asking "Is anyone home?" Teachers cannot display their anger through acts of unkindness and expect anyone in their class to give them the respect they demand. Often you get what you give. Sarcasm has no place in a learning environment. Teachers must leave their personal issues and baggage out of the classroom.

Many teachers see the grade they give on an assignment as the ultimate feedback. The truth is students seldom get any feedback from a mark. A grade shows them where they stand in a range of marks but does not show them how to improve. Some students will work diligently for a good mark, others could care less. Watch how your students react when you give back an assignment with a grade on it. The students with great marks will immediately check with others to see how they compare. The struggling students will look at the grade, and either crumple the assignment up and throw it out or stuff it into the deep corners of the desk.

If you do not give students proper feedback then you cannot

expect to see improvement or growth. **No feedback equals no growth. Comments for improvement, coached in a positive tone, give the students a feeling of hope and a desire to improve. This climate of support needs to be established from day one.**

The first week of school is the time for you to begin to establish your role as the person who will assist with student learning. During this time you must show the students that their education and ability to be successful is near and dear to your heart. The students need to know that you believe in them and that you see great potential in what they can achieve. You must know that all students can succeed. If you don't believe this, you must ask yourself these questions, "Why am I a teacher," "Why have I chosen this profession?"

Introducing Subjects: The Hook

You want your students to know that when they enter your class it is a place of work. It only makes sense that on your first day you begin to work. This should be the time when you introduce your timetable and the various subjects you will be covering. The curriculum should never be a secret, something only teachers know about. Students need to know what they are going to be exposed to during the school year. They need to be aware how you are going to assess their performance. By doing this early, the students begin to feel comfortable because they can see that you are organized and that you have a sense of direction. If you don't have a plan, if you don't know where you are going, how do you expect your students to have a sense of direction?

I have worked with many teachers over my thirty-year career. Most of them had excellent long-range plans and an awareness of where they were leading their class with the curriculum. They would arrive early and stay late to be prepared for the students. Occasionally, you would find them in the school on the weekends, planning and preparing work for the week to follow. These teachers often planned days in advance. I have also worked with teachers who were never prepared to teach. They had no working knowledge of the curriculum, nor did they have strategies for the delivery of the lessons. They could be seen running down the hall to the photocopy machine, to run off a worksheet, while chaos was breaking loose in the class. Often they entered school with the bell and chased the school buses down the road at the end of the day. Again, you get what you give in this profession. You must be prepared.

The introduction of concepts, skills, subjects or themes needs to be something you have thought out in advance. The way you introduce a topic can have a severe influence on how your class will respond to working in that subject. As I mentioned earlier, you are the master manipulator. Your enthusiasm and energy is contagious. The passion you show the students is often transferred to them. Students need to know why they are doing something. They need to see the connections to their real world because they want to know how they will use these skills.

Your passion towards teaching and the material you are covering plays a critical role in the level of engagement of your students. The students will be listening, very carefully, to the way you introduce them to new learning. They will feed off your enthusiasm and confidence.

Several years ago, I had the privilege of listening to to Erin Gruwell speak at a conference in Toronto. Erin Gruwell was from Long Beach, California, and was the inspiration behind the movie "Freedom Writers." While listening to her emotional presentation, I was astounded by the impact that Anne Frank's "The Diary of a Young Girl" had had on her students. Erin Gruwell's class consisted of many students who had experienced difficult lives as a result of gangs, gang violence, domestic violence and so on. I wanted to return to my school and introduce this book to my students and to explore the relationship it had to students with difficulties. I knew I had to sell this concept to my students. The key to their engagement was my enthusiasm and passion. I was still filled with excitement when I told the students of my experiences with to Erin Gruwell and the Freedom Writers. I showed them a short video of Erin Gruwell. My students were pulled into the emotions of the students in her class, as they spoke of how she had changed their lives. They listened carefully as each student discussed the impact that Anne Frank's diary had on them, and I could see tears in my students' eyes as they watched young men cry as they told their personal stories. I introduced the diary to the class and suggested we read it in teams, giving them a better opportunity to share their feelings in a smaller group. I asked that we identify one essential question that we would try to answer as we read the book. The question we decided on was, "What is in 'The Diary of a Young Girl' that would change the lives of these students in Long Beach, California?" I cannot describe the energy created in the class for the next several weeks. The responses I received to the essential question went further than I could have dreamed. My passion and excitement created enthusiasm within my class. It all started with me and it ended with the students.

My last few years of teaching involved utilizing "experiential education" as a learning strategy. There are many definitions of this teaching approach; however, for the purpose of this book I describe experiential education as an approach that actively engages students in their learning through direct interaction with real world connections. Experiential learning requires the students to play an active role in the experiences and those experiences are followed by reflection as a method of processing, understanding and making sense of them. Chapter Six will discuss this approach to teaching in greater detail.

During my years using experiential education, I would spend a good amount of time coaching students with their independent research projects. I showed them the importance of using a "hook" when showing their understanding to other students. The ability to pull your audience into your presentation is a critical factor to consider when making various presentations. This is also true for teaching.

To engage students in learning, we often need to hook them, to grab their attention and to make them want to buy in.

One Size Does Not Fit All

> In a time of drastic change, it is the learners who inherit the future. The learned find themselves equipped to live in a world that no longer exists.
>
> **—Eric Hoffer**

We have to teach our students how to learn. The world in which they will enter upon completion of school is much different than our world. It will be one of constant change and filled with an endless need to develop new skills. Tony Wagner in his book entitled, "The Global Achievement Gap: Why Even Our Best Schools Don't Teach The New Survival Skills Our Children Need - And What We Can Do About It," outlines the needs of students in the world today. The skills required for success in the 21st century are much different from the skills required by past generations. Global awareness, financial literacy, creativity, innovation, critical thinking, problem solving, communication and collaboration are just some of the skills that will be required to meet success both in the world of work and as citizens.

The graduates today will need to be flexible, adaptable and self-directed as they navigate through the unsettled water of the new economic realities facing the world today. To be successful, students need to know who they are as learners and how they learn best. They need to know how to use their strengths and how to improve their weaknesses. They have to see learning as part of life and as a significant part of their future.

Importance of Caring

The caring for every student is such an important part of teaching. Not only must students care about their learning, they must also feel safe in their learning environment. A student has to feel valued.

As a teacher we hold the power to make or break a student. Their future as a learner lies in our hands. In India there is a saying that "all you become is because of your teachers." I have given this statement a great deal of thought and I believe that not only do teachers hold such control over what our students become, I also believe we share the same responsibility for what they don't become. I am aware that there are many factors beyond our control that influence the destiny and future of our students; however, as teachers we have the power and calling to assist in every way to help them with the steps required to be successful. Any student I have had that I was not successful with was because I did not try hard enough to address their needs. Some will say that a statement like that carries unnecessary responsibility for a teacher, but I say if you are not prepared for that responsibility then you have chosen the wrong profession.

**In some student's lives, we are the only person who can make
a difference and give them that chance to succeed. Yes, it is a
heavy load. Get used to it.**

As teachers we want to create a positive learning environment
where all of our students will be successful. We use differentiated
instruction and assessment as key elements in our classrooms.
Being aware of how our students learn and how they display their
understanding is critical as we guide them up the educational
mountain. If we agree that students have different combinations
of learning styles, multiple intelligences, and decision-making
styles, and other varying attributes, then it makes perfect sense
that we must address these differences when we present students
with new ideas and skills. Differentiation and assessment will be
discussed in greater detail in later chapters.

Their individual needs have to be addressed if we expect all of
out students to meet success. However, there is so much more to
creating a positive classroom experience than simply being aware
of how our students learn. We must create a learning environment where all students feel accepted and where they can be safe
and comfortable to face new learning experiences. We must give
students the opportunity to be valued team members, to be able
to freely express their opinions, to make mistakes, to take risks
and simply to be themselves.

Creating an environment that allows students to learn in ways
that are unique to them involves careful planning on a daily basis.
The key to every positive classroom begins with us, the teachers.
Our students must know in their hearts that we are pleased to
have them in our classrooms. Greeting our students daily as they
enter our rooms creates a welcoming start to the day. A friendly
smile starts our day on a positive note. It is very important we
know how are students are feeling because they often tow with
them the baggage of life which occurred outside school. This may
have a serious impact on how the day will progress. Gauging student temperament may be accomplished during a morning circle

discussion where each student is given the opportunity to share how he/she is feeling about the upcoming day. When we allow our students to open up (and give them the right to opt out of the discussion if they so desire), we create an atmosphere of caring. I never miss the opportunity to jump into the discussion and share how I am feeling about the day to come. Let them see you as a real person, beyond the walls of the school. Avoid personal details but embrace vulnerability. You will build a strong and sensitive learning community.

It is also important that we know what interests our students in and out of school. The more we understand, the better we will be to meet their needs.

The establishment of trust with your students is critical to creating a positive learning environment. They need to know that they can trust us and more importantly, that we trust them. Give them opportunities to express ideas and hear those of their classmates. Weekly student-led classroom meetings and monthly divisional meetings encourage them to accept responsibility for what is happening around them. There, they voice concerns and find positive solutions to various classroom scenarios. Giving the students responsibility to set the agenda, establish the meeting norms and freely discuss concerns, demonstrates a belief in their abilities and a respect for what they have to say.

I like to laugh, tell stories and have fun. That is my in my nature. I always manage to have a good time regardless of what I do. My entire teaching career was filled with joy and laughter. I liked to play with my students and they could see the how much I enjoyed being with them. My classroom was often filled with laughter. Your sense of humour can be used effectively with your students. Although there is a fine line between having fun and being silly, when used to your advantage, storytelling and humour can create a relaxed and open learning environment.

School should not be a boring place filled with textbooks, notes and tests. Students should want to be in your class because they are comfortable in your presence. Many times my students would sit totally engaged as I would tell them a story from my past. Often, I would talk about something from my youth that was funny, such as the day my head foamed up in the rain after using my Dad's Resdan hair product. The more the students saw me as a real person, the more comfortable they were around me. My students developed excellent listening skills as I would intentionally "ramble on." Often at the conclusion of my tale I would ask the students to recount where I had gone with my story. Each of them could repeat in detail every word I spoke. To them I was a story teller, to me I was developing good listening habits. You can never underestimate the power of being yourself. From my experience, students can easily spot a fake. If you are trying to be something other than who you really are the students will notice. Be yourself, get the job done but have fun while you do it.

We can never underestimate the power of positive reinforcement. All students are different when it comes to being acknowledged for doing something well. Some are very pleased to have their successes shared with the entire class, while others prefer that praise be given privately. Often a quiet whisper, expressing how pleased we are, will create a lasting impression in our student's minds. Carefully slipping a congratulatory note to an unsuspecting student will create a response far beyond your expectations.

We should never miss an opportunity to be positive with our students. It is the cornerstone to building a solid classroom foundation.

Our students spend a considerable amount of time in our

classrooms. We must believe that each one of them can learn. To accomplish this, we must begin by creating an environment that gives them the opportunities to safely explore their learning. It is our job to be there for each of our students and it is our responsibility to protect them and guide them as they move forward. Our kindness and our guiding hand will be remembered long after they have moved beyond our schools.

Importance of Consistency

Say what you mean and mean what you say.

Students need to know that you are consistently real and that what you do and say today will be the same tomorrow. Never promise something you can't deliver on and don't make threats that you are not prepared to carry out. It does not take your students long to learn your game. They know very early in the first week or so of school how consistent you are.

Consistency applies to everything from application of the class rules and routines to the acceptance of quality work. Your credibility is closely linked to your consistency and the sincerity of your caring. Teaching is a complex business that can be made that much easier when you have these qualities firmly in place.

It takes very little time for a student to see through an idle threat. So many times we hear teachers saying, "If you do that one more time," or " I have had enough, the next time you will…" When consequences are not attached and immediately applied to a threat it makes the threat unworthy of attention. Fred Jones (Positive Classroom Discipline) describes this situation as "opening your mouth and slitting your throat." If you have no intentions of giving a consequence, then don't make the threat. Think about what behaviour you want stopped. Give a specific direction to the students. If you feel a consequence is warranted and the students do not comply, then you must follow through immediately. You have no choice. Your credibility is on the line.

Rapport with Parent / Making the First Contact

During the first few days of school, or in some cases prior to the beginning of classes, you need to make a contact with the parents. This contact is very important. Most parents want to know who you are. You will be the person their child will be talking about every evening. This initial contact can help you establish a positive relationship with the parents. Your goal throughout the year is to maintain that relationship, thus creating a successful partnership between you, the student and the home. The parents don't need to be your best friend, in fact, you don't want them to be that close. Remember, what you want is a positive, professional relationship with your students' parents.

The establishment of this first contact can be done in many ways. A letter home on the first day can outline who you are, your expectation for the students and some of the things you hope your class will accomplish through the year or term. This is a good time to discuss your plans and goals. By doing this effectively, you are establishing, from the beginning, that you are organized, prepared and that you are interested in having a positive relationship with the parents.

Teachers can also phone the parents. The same goals can be achieved. This is not always easy to do, as many parents work and cannot always be reached, however, this contact can be very valuable because it is much more personal. An open house or open invitation to come in and meet you during the first week of school can also be a very important way of building a teacher and parent partnership. Throughout the term it is important to maintain this positive contact. There will be times when you need to call the parents to discuss situations that are not always positive.

Don't forget that contact can be made for reasons other than reporting negative situations. A phone call or a note to say you are proud of something that has happened can be very beneficial and can pay major dividends down the road.

First Day Interruptions

Always be prepared for the unexpected on the first day of school. There will be new students you hadn't planned on. There will be those who do not show up. There will be knocks on your door and requests from administration for numbers and details. There will be forms and paper work, parents calling, staff meetings, timetable changes, moving students from filled classes, tears, laughter. Don't worry, you will survive and sleep very well when you finally close your eyes for a well-deserved rest. The first day and the first week are very busy and very important. You must plan to do it right. What you establish in the beginning will be the groundwork for the rest of the year. **Like a Boy Scout...Be Prepared.**

Chapter Three
Classroom Management

There are as many ways to solve a behaviour problem as there are behaviour problems. It is easier to prevent a situation than it is to solve it. By using effective teaching and classroom management strategies, most behaviour issues can be eliminated before they begin. How you set up your class, the rapport you develop with your students, the way you design lessons for success, the depth of student engagement and your consistency when applying procedures in the class are all key to creating positive classroom management.

I cannot underestimate the importance of common sense when working with your students. Your students are real, just like you. Their needs and wants are just like yours, after all, we are all human beings with basic goals in life such as being safe and respected.

Not all students are the same. Each pupil in your class is different. They learn differently, they like to be reinforced differently and they need to be managed differently. Problems occur when we refuse to recognize student differences. Our goals, our routines and our rules do apply to everyone. How we get them to follow your objectives depends largely on you and how you effectively engage them in the learning process.

There are a few basic types of students. One type comes to school prepared to learn, self-motivated and ready to be engaged. These students are like sponges and soak up everything we have to offer. These are the students who go home at night and share at the dinner table the wonderful experiences they had at school. They are usually happy, energetic and involved in school and school activities. I have experienced these students over the years and have been blessed by their presence in my class.

Students at the other extreme see school as a waste of their time. They are there because they have to be. They are usually unmotivated, unskilled and often have many gaps in their learning experiences. These students can range from loud and outspoken to quiet and withdrawn. The students who fall in the middle group are motivated at times, engaged at times and complete most assignments at times. They can do better, and they know it, but they have been doing okay so far, so why the need to expend more effort? There are other students who fill in the gray areas. These are students who try very hard to succeed yet still struggle to meet the standards. There are the gifted and talented and some who are chronic underachievers. Some students have identified learning difficulties and work very hard to make small gains. All students are different in the way they interact with their learning. We need to recognize their individuality.

Some students respond effectively to open praise. You can share their successes with the class. You can use them as examples and you can tell them how proud you are of their hard work. These pupils will respond accordingly by repeating the behaviour you praised. Other students don't want to be addressed publicly. They prefer your praise in a more private setting. A note or a quick and quiet conversation is great for them.

One of your biggest challenges as a teacher is to find out what makes your students "tick." What are their needs, what are their wants, what has real meaning to them and how you reinforce their behaviour. How can you best establish a positive, caring rapport with them which allows them to feel safe enough with you to move forward? You want every student in your class to think that you are there just for them.

There is no greater feeling as a teacher than when you have connected with your students. There is only one way to accomplish this...talk to them.

I recall a young student I taught in grade seven who struggled with learning and with behaviour. I found myself desperately searching for something, anything, I could praise him for. When the opportunity did arise, I pounced on it with the force of a tiger. I stopped the class and proudly acknowledged his accomplishments. This was an enlightening moment for me as a new teacher. I watched in horror as this young boy's behaviour rapidly declined to the point that he was eventually removed from the class and sent home for a few days. Not all students respond the way you think they will. This student was telling me that he could not and would not accept praise from me in front of the class. We talked when he returned and together we came up with a solution. If I was so inclined on telling him I was proud, then it had to be done quietly and without the class knowing. That was over twenty-five years ago. To this day, that student and I have an incredible rapport. I have taught his children and I still never miss an opportunity to tell him how proud I am of him—quietly, mind you.

Several years ago I received a letter from a student I had taught in my third year of teaching. I remember her as a wonderful child who sat directly in front of my desk. She was going through a difficult time at home as her parents were separating. She told me she had wanted to write me several times but could never find the right time. The letter explained that she had been doing a lot of reflecting about her past. She often thought about my "lectures" to the class of what life would be like for them beyond school. Through my inexperience as a teacher, I had told them that life was a jungle out there. Like many students, she didn't understand what I meant about that. Not many thirteen year olds could. It wasn't until she turned twenty-five, married and with children that she fully understood the message I was trying to pass on to them. She thanked me for my honesty and told me that she had never met a teacher that was so open, so honest and so caring. She continued to thank me for the support I gave her while she was in my class. She could never bring herself to come back and see me and visit out of the fear that she would have to face the fact that I was there for other students as well. She had always hung on to the idea that I was there just for her. To this day I still read that letter from time to time and it always brings tears to my eyes. Kindness and caring is always returned to us many times over.

Working the Crowd

We have discussed the importance of setting up your class so you can freely and efficiently move about the room. A teacher is very effective when they "work the crowd." Teaching through movement is great on many levels. First and most importantly is it keeps the students interested in you. For some, it is an interest in what you are saying, for others, it is an interest in where you are and where you are going. When you teach physically planted at the front of the room, you are sending a message that you are on a stage, you are the show. Many students will tune you out very quickly and those in the far reaches of the room may even grab a few winks. Behaviour issues occur on the fringe. Students engage in conversation, doodle, pass notes, look out the window, text message friends in other classes. You get the point. They don't always want to pay attention to what is happening on the stage. Therefore, it makes sense to move about as you teach, talking and sharing as you travel about the room. You can see what they are doing and they know it. The need to be more attentive increases and accountability escalates. You are free to teach and discuss from the "hot spots" in the room. This is one on the most fundamental and basic classroom management techniques. Simple and cost effective.

During my thirty years of teaching I went through several pairs of shoes. What I found was that the sole of my right shoe always wore out long before the left sole. I could never fully understand why this was happening. Being a creative teacher and always looking for a way to engage my students, I asked them to help me solve the "mystery of the right shoe." After some deep problem solving discussions, the students came to me with the answer to the mystery. I never sat down as a teacher. I was always moving around the class as I worked with students. I moved as I taught, I walked as I demonstrated. Never did I stay in one place for long. Being on my feet was part of the problem, however, the reason for the right sole wearing out quicker than the other had to do with the direction I moved in. According to my students, I always walked in a clockwise motion, turning on my right foot as I worked the crowd. Kids can be so observant. They see everything we do and know exactly where we are at all times.

Creating Independence

Some students love to dominate a teacher's time. If you do the math, you will see that thirty students during a sixty-minute class should get about two minutes each of your personal time. Our classes are filled with what Fred Jones (Positive Classroom Discipline) calls "weeners." These are the students in your class that are totally helpless and cannot function without you. You are their life support system. They are always close to you, their hands are always up, they are always asking questions, they want reassurance and they want your time. In addition to these "weeners" there is a group of "weener wantabees" who are waiting to take up pole position with you. Although these students are usually well-meaning, they do pose a serious problem to classroom management.

If some students are dominating your time, then what are the others doing while you are occupied?

The solution to this situation is simple, yet complex, at the same time. You have to ween them off you and make them self-sufficient, something you want for all your students. You want your class to be filled with independent workers. To do this, you must structure your lessons so that every student is aware of what to do next. This can be done by using step by step visuals during your lesson presentation. When these students need your help you only need to check where they are, praise what they have done well, prompt them to move to the next step and leave so they can do this on their own. This way the "weeners" are being trained to be independent and you are not letting them dominate your time.

With older classes, I institute a system where a student had steps to follow before asking me for help. I teach a lesson by breaking the concept into manageable steps. As I am introducing the skills or concept, I record each step, with an example, on the front board or on chart paper. I want the students to use this as a guide. Students who are experiencing difficulty, should check the board to see what the next step should be. If that is not helping them to understand then they are to ask one member of their group. If that too was unsuccessful then they could ask anyone in their group. If this last stage did not assist them then I would help. I would ask them first if they followed the stages. As a teacher, it tells me all I need to know when no one in the group can help...I taught a bad lesson and I need to re-teach in another way. The chances are, this group is not alone. Many times we want to blame our students for not "getting it." That isn't always fair to the students. Often, I found that I failed to teach the concept in a way that addressed the individual learning styles of my students. The problem can often be overcome by additional examples and visual backup for the students.

Designing a Lesson for Independence - The Hook, The Skill, Consolidation

An effective lesson has three distinct parts, each designed to help the student move forward towards independent application of the skills taught. The first stage involves engaging the learners by creating an interest in the subject or topic. You need to find out what the students know about the concept. You need to get them excited. All students want to know why they need to know this concept or have this skill. The second stage involves acquisition of the specific skills. This is done through explanations, examples and modelling. During this stage the students are given questions to work with, thus allowing them to practice their understanding while you watch. It is during this structured practice stage that all misunderstanding should be corrected. This can only be accomplished through direct observation. You may need to re-teach to ensure the concept has been grasped. The final stage involves consolidating the skills or concept. At this point you want to "fine tune" the concept or skill by providing guided practice. Your role as the teacher changes from instructor to that of a coach. As the students work on their assignments, you will be offering corrective feedback. By doing this, the students will be able to move forward into independent practice where they should be able to discriminate errors and self-correct when needed. Finally, in this stage, the students should be exposed to variations in the concept, allowing them to further develop their understanding through generalization.

Awareness of the different learning styles has to be at the forefront of your mind as you prepare. Differentiation of instruction is critical if you are going to meet the needs of all students in your class.

The days of having all of them open a textbook to page 43, read, summarize and answer the questions should have all but disappeared. Unfortunately in many schools this remains as the primary teaching strategy. Through careful planning and awareness of your student's learning styles, you can create a lesson where all students have the opportunity to grasp the material you are presenting. Lesson design is one of the key components of a well-managed classroom. Many behaviour issues occur as a result of poor classroom instruction. Students don't understand because it is not being presented in a way that engages them. They can't work independently, because they don't know what to do. All students **can** learn and **will** learn if lessons are presented in a way that meets their individual needs.

Hooking the Learner

This is the most critical stage of teaching. A student needs to buy into what you are teaching. They have to see the relevance of this topic and see how it fits into their understanding of the world. Your enthusiasm and passion are contagious. It doesn't take a student long to see how you feel about what you are teaching. You need to make the students believe that what you are about to introduce to them is real, relevant and worth their time. I know this is a challenge but the payoff is invaluable. The students are asking themselves the following questions:

1. Why should I know this?

2. How does this relate to what I already know?

3. What is it you want me to be able to do with this?

Acquiring the skills

Once the students see the relevance of what they are about to study, the next stage is the introduction of the topic and the related skills needed for success. The topic should be presented in a variety of ways to meet the learning styles of your students. Auditory information needs to be reinforced with visual cues. Diagrams, charts, videos and computer sites are important tools to use during the skill acquisition stage. When possible, the students should also be given the opportunity to explore the topic using a tactile, hands-on experience. You must be aware of every learner in your class when presenting a new topic or a new skill. Doing this will help increase student understanding and engagement. As a teacher, you should do the following:

1, Explain the concept in a variety of ways

2. Show specific examples, exemplars and models

3. Give opportunity to practice; and

4. Allow time to discuss and share understanding

Consolidation, Grasping the Concept

The consolidation stage is where the students begin to show their understanding of the newly acquired information. At the completion, the student should be able to demonstrate a competent understanding and be able to apply this understanding in other areas of the curriculum. It is not enough that the students are given the opportunity to rehearse their understanding, you must also be there to make sure that their practice is perfect practice. This is the time to reinforce knowledge and correct misunderstanding through positive, corrective feedback. Once you are sure there is good understanding, you should provide opportunities for the students to show their understanding and to share what they have learned. As a mentor or coach, you should do the following:

1. Provide guided practice experience where you monitor their progress

2. Design assignments to show application of understanding

3. Create experiences for independent practice using the skills

The Independent Learner

The ideal students have developed the attitude and skills to work independently. They should be able to answer many of their own questions and should thrive on positive feedback from the teacher. They can effectively evaluate the validity of the resources they use, suspend judgement, ask critical questions, formulate an opinion and display their understanding in a way that is unique to them. None of this happens without direct intervention of the teacher. We can never assume that students will develop these skills on their own.

Everything must be taught in a way that makes sense to the student. All students must make an inner connection with themselves, before success can be achieved. As they move forward in their learning, the students will begin to develop understanding on their own. This is what we all should strive for as life long learners.

Managing Off-Task Behaviour

Behaviour issues always come before teaching.

When a situation arises in your class, you must deal with that issue immediately. You cannot successfully teach when something negative is happening around you. Many situations can be dealt with quietly and privately by simply moving into that area of the room to teach. A quiet whisper followed by a thank you for compliance can often head off further escalation of behaviour. Many students do not want their behaviour to be put on stage for all of the class to view and therefore being sensitive and caring can often help eliminate future behaviours. On occasion, you may need to deal with an issue in a more aggressive manner, with the possibility of consequences for continued behaviour. Remember to be reasonable but consistent. It is not about getting even or punishing. It is about eliminating a behaviour and having everyone involved win. The teacher gets the behaviour to stop, the students feel safe and valued.

Years ago, there was a commercial on television for Fram Oil Filters. The slogan for the ad was, "Pay me now or pay me later." Basically what it was saying was that if you pay attention to the small things up front then you won't have to pay the big costs caused by your delays at a later time. This philosophy holds true in education and classroom management. Don't put off for later what you must do now. Discipline comes before instruction, meaning that if there is a behaviour issue in your class, you must end your teaching and deal with it. The message you are sending to your students is that you will not accept poor behaviour and you will not teach over it.

You are saying, very clearly, that in my class I expect your attention and will stop at nothing to get it.

Let's say you have created this wonderful lesson plan and just as you begin to work your way through the presentation you notice that a few of your students are off task, chatting with each other or playing with objects at their desks. Your first action should be to move into their space and continue to teach from there. It should become very evident if they are responding to your presence. If they do, then great. Camp out for a while in that area, then move on. You have addressed the situation without even opening your mouth. If the situation continues, then you must stop what you are doing and deal with this. Initially, you want your confrontation to be quiet and private. This is between you and them. There is no need to give them or yourself an audience. Speak to them in a quiet voice and tell them what you want them to be doing. If the students comply, thank them, hang around in their area for a while as you return to the lesson. Think of the messages you are sending to the rest of the class. One, I will move into your space to let you know that I am aware of what you are doing. Two, I will stop teaching if you remain off task. Three, I will keep this issue between you and I and give you a chance to comply without an open confrontation and fourthly and most importantly, I will thank you for your cooperation because I respect the fact that you have done as I asked.

It is very important to deal with a small situation immediately, quietly and calmly. What you really want is to get through your instructions and put the students to work. You don't have the time, nor the energy, to engage in open combat over every issue. Keep it small and keep it quiet.

There is also a saying that tells you not to sweat the small stuff. A teacher's definition of small stuff varies. What one teacher will deal with another will ignore. To me, a small issue becomes a bigger issue when it prevents the student or other students from learning. In the beginning of the year, it is important for you to address the "small stuff" when you are trying to establish routines, and more importantly, your consistency as their teacher. A student may interpret your lack of attention to an issue as permission to change the rules. Remember the importance of saying what you mean and meaning what you say. Your students are always watching you to see if the rules still apply. For some reason, they believe that teachers change their minds over time. Perhaps this is a result of them getting their way at home by being persistent.

Your persistence has to be better than theirs.

Students have become masters of finding the loop holes. You will always be surprised at how creative your students will be at circumnavigating your plans. Be as clear and specific as you can and anticipate the unexpected.

Chapter Four
Behaviour Management

I have had the privilege of working with hundreds of students throughout my thirty years as a teacher and I look back at each and every one of them with the warmest of thoughts. Not all of them were perfect—in fact, few were; however, each one of them was special in his/her own way. I had my share of challenging students who didn't always see education the same way I did. There were those who refused to work, those who craved the attention of negative behaviour and others who just saw school as play time. Regardless of how they viewed me and my expectations, I had one main goal and that was to create a positive learning environment where they, as individuals, could feel safe.

The point is, when dealing with behavioural issues, your job as a teacher, as the adult in the class, is to protect them. I know this may sound strange when a student is acting out and challenging your authority, however, by protecting them you are showing how deeply you care.

Behavioural issues range from small, easy to fix, to situations that are large scale and require actions beyond the classroom. The small issues are yours to deal with. It is your actions and the way you confront the situation that will continue to establish your credibility. You are the manager of your room and it is your job to deal with these smaller behaviours. The moment you ask someone else to deal with your problem, you have lessened your credibility. It is like Mom saying, "I won't deal with this, you wait until your father gets home." All of us who have experienced this in our home lives know that we grew up to fear and respect Dad and recognize Mom as a pushover. We knew that what Dad said was law but Mom's word was questionable because she wouldn't follow through on her own. She needed Dad to be the heavy. This applies to you and your class. Sending students to the office for things like failure to do work, talking out or being out of their seats shows your students that you can't deal with the small issues. **You** need to be the heavy. You need to be the person they are accountable to. You need to dole out the consequences and you need to supervise these consequences. Your students have to be accountable to themselves and to you first.

Too often teachers will use the principal as their first line of defence. I have witnessed this firsthand, over the last few years of my career, when I was placed in a position of designated teacher when the administration was out of the building. This is the teacher who acts on the principal's behalf while they are out of the school. Many students were sent to the office for minor infractions. There are many problems with this. The most important being the loss of credibility for the classroom teacher. When a teacher abdicates responsibility for a student's behaviour they are also giving up control of future behavioural problems. Things will always get worse when this happens. Secondly, the office is an active place. Principals are very busy with the day-to-day activities involved in running a school. Often, they have very little time to give to "small" behaviour issues. When they do take the responsibility for dealing with behaviour, the teachers must be aware of the fact that they have passed this situation over to someone else. Teachers don't always like the decisions made by administrators when dealing with misbehaving students. The situation is this, once you give up ownership, you also give up the right to question the consequences.

Many times I would see students standing outside the office door. When I would ask them why they were there, I would be presented with a variety of answers, ranging from, "I don't know" to "The teacher sent me because I am a colour blue now on the chart." I never really knew what the teacher's expectations were of me. The time it took to get to the real reason was unbelievable. Once I discovered the "why," I was then confused about what they wanted me to do with these small infractions. I was never really sure what purpose all of this was serving. Certainly, the student wasn't benefiting nor was the teacher. If you must send a student to the office, contact the office first and explain the reason for the referral. Make it very clear what your expectations are.

There are some situations that are beyond your control. These are usually behaviours that put a student or other students at risk. It may be a verbal threat or physical violence or some illegal activity. It could be an action that is in violation of a behaviour policy outlined by legislation. Regardless of what the issue is, these types of actions require the intervention of a higher authority. It is mandatory for the safety of that student and the safety of others to pass on responsibility. These situations do not challenge your credibility. Explain to your students that there are situations out of your control and for the protection of all, you can't be involved. They will respect you for that.

There can be times when a very dangerous situation can arise. On the rare occasion, a student will lose control. Some become verbally aggressive, others resort to physical violence directed towards classmates, the teacher or themselves. When this happens you must call for help immediately.

Protecting everyone in the class is your first priority.

Often, it is wise to get all of the students out of the class, if possible. The student that is losing control does not need an audience. Call on your colleagues for assistance. This can be a very delicate situation and needs to be handled with care. Never try to deal with this situation alone. Your administration must be there for the protection of everyone involved. Once the situation is under control, document everything that happened while it is still fresh in your mind.

You Need To Keep It Small and Private

The most important thing you want to do when dealing with inappropriate behaviour is keep the situation small and away from an audience. You want to keep the discussion between you and the student.

The student needs the opportunity to comply while saving face with his or her peers.

The moment you make the situation public, you have put the student in a position where the peer group takes on importance. It is difficult for some students to comply when they know their friends are watching. Once the class becomes the audience, the situation will escalate quickly. You may find yourself in a verbal tennis match, where each challenge by the student is met by an increased challenge by you. Before long, the situation is out of control and what was small has become huge. Your authority has been questioned and you have to respond. The problem is you have many eyes watching and learning from this experience. You have failed to protect the student and as a result you now have a bigger problem to deal with. You can very quickly lose the trust of your students. You must be seen as a role model by your students.

The character you display when dealing with conflict should act as an example of how to handle a situation in a positive manner.

It is always easier to be proactive than to have a situation get to the point where you must be reactive. You must be alert to everything that is happening around you. If you see the beginning of something starting, you must move in to the situation and let your presence be felt. The student needs to know that you are aware and that you are prepared to respond, if necessary. Often just being in the area is enough to head off potential misbehaviour. Quietly, thank the student and move on. Many situations usually escalate because of the lack of initial intervention. An example could be a disagreement you observe in a small group between two students. If the argument is ignored without you moving in, the possibility of it getting out of control is probable. The students will distract other team members and eventually no one will be on-task. A simple solution is for you to move into the group, quietly intervene and suggest a solution such as the students sharing their concerns with you in private. The advantage of moving into the situation quickly is that it eliminates an audience and gives the students a chance to get it under control before it gets out of hand. You are giving the students the chance to own the problem and solve it before it becomes big. You are also showing the class that when your expectations are not being followed, you will be there to help them continue in a positive way. Don't allow yourself to be pulled into time-consuming situations where the rest of the class is out of your view. You have to be aware of as much as possible. That is not to say that things won't happen without you knowing. Believe me, the students are very good at hiding what is going on. You will be blindsided at times. It happens, just accept it.

There is debate over thanking students for doing what is expected. It can be argued that compliance is a given and that to respond with a thank you is redundant. I see this as a simple act of courtesy and kindness.

Why Consequences? The Importance of Fairness

Long before children enter school, they are aware that negative behaviour has a consequence. All parents, whether skilled or not, have ways of letting their child know this. A student who misbehaves in class is very much aware that there will be a consequence.

It is always important to keep fairness as the key to discipline. It is not our job to punish students.

Our goal should be to help them learn from the experience and show them the correct way of doing something. A consequence can be a negative response to a negative behaviour or it can be used effectively to create a positive learning experience. The days of writing lines has long since disappeared. What does a student really learn from writing "I will not be bad" a hundred times? We are in the business of education, helping students to learn. There is no learning involved in writing lines. I have witnessed teachers having students write dictionary pages. When the student didn't comply, they were given additional pages. Before long the student and the teacher were in an impossible situation. Nobody was going to win and the student certainly wasn't learning. There is an old saying, "Open your mouth and slit your throat." Basically what this means is that you are accountable for what you say. Unless you are prepared to follow through then watch what you say. Remember, your credibility is on the line. Be fair and be reasonable when you are deciding on a consequence. You want the student to learn from this.

I recall talking with a colleague of mine several years ago whose son was experiencing great difficulties in school. His child was having a hard time getting his homework completed. The teacher was also very frustrated, and as a punishment, had decided to double the work load for every assignment incomplete. Needless to say, the homework continued to be ignored by the student. The situation had gone out of control long before a parent meeting was set up. The meeting was a disaster. The consequences were so unreasonable that the teacher could no longer justify the punishment. No student could ever dig themselves out of the "hole" the teacher had made for them. No one could be expected to get caught up on the amount of work that was given as a consequence. Be reasonable and make it a learning experience. We are not in the business of punishment.

Teachers need to choose their battles. Not all off-task situations need to be addressed. If the students are not physically, emotionally or morally hurting each other, or if they are not disturbing others, it may not necessarily require your intervention. Certain types of behaviour are not negotiable and when these situations arise we need to be firm, consistent yet flexible. The way we deal with one student may not work for another. We want the actions to stop, but we need to be creative in choosing our methods. We must look at discipline as teaching with the ultimate goal being self-discipline.

A school I worked in had a rule regarding students wearing hoodies during class. Hoodies are the part of a sweatshirt that can be pulled up over your head. The policy was created along the same principle as wearing a hat in school. A student in the class next door decided she would challenge this rule and came to class with her hood raised. Her teacher asked the student to remove the hood and she refused to do so. Immediately, war was declared and the battle had begun. The student was told to leave the room and return only when she could follow the rules of the school. Now on the surface this may sound like a logical course of action. What the teacher failed to understand was that this student was prepared to win the war at all costs. After two weeks of the student sitting against the wall outside the room, it was becoming apparent to all of us watching this event that some new strategy had to be employed. Neither the teacher nor the student was going to win unless someone took a step towards a resolution. One of the combatants was an adult and it seemed perfectly logical that the teacher would make the first step. That was not to be in this case as the teacher saw a retreat on her decision as a weakness and a loss of credibility. Eventually, the principal had to intervene and after a long debate, the student returned to the class, hoodie still on.

This situation is an example of what can happen when we react to a situation without understanding what lead up to the incident. When we react immediately, we are not giving the student the opportunity to explain their actions. In the case, the student was given a hair cut by a family member the night before. Not having any training in hair styling, the cut was less than desirable and very embarrassing for the student. She debated whether to come to school or stay home until the hair grew. She decided to come to class but to cover her head with her hoodie to avoid ridicule. Not being a strong student, nor very fond of school, she immediately regarded the teacher's reaction as negative and refused to explain her situation. This entire problem could have been dealt with in a positive way that protected the child; instead, it spiralled out of control. The teacher lost the credibility she wanted to protect by overreacting. The student became empowered which resulted in further situations involving the teacher and student. It is critical that we think before we react. We need to understand what lies behind a behaviour before we issue a consequence. It is easy to give a consequence for a behaviour, but it is much more effective to find a way to be positive and avoid the negative behaviour completely.

Appropriate and immediate positive consequences can make behaviour more frequent. Similarly, increasing positive incentives can lead to a decrease in problem behaviour. By providing a positive consequence for cooperative behaviour we can often steer our students away from problem behaviour. This may involve giving students extra privileges, extra attention from others, praise or access to a desirable activity. Teachers need to be aware that positive reinforcement can lead to increased negative behaviour. If a student's goal is attention from his/hers peers or from the adults in the room, he/she may continue the behaviour as a way to secure that attention. We must be aware of the agenda behind the behaviour. All students should be praised when they are behaving in an acceptable way. It is much easier to encourage good behaviour than it is to discipline poor behaviour. Being proactive is much better than being reactive. We should never hesitate to stop work when we witness positive behaviour. By doing this, you are pointing out to the students that you notice their cooperation and want everyone to be aware that it is appreciated.

The Repeat Offender

Not all students are prepared to follow the routines and rules of your class. Some will not accept the way you want them to do things and often these students will not react positively to your fair and reasonable consequences. You will be saying to them often that we have been through all of this. These students are repeat offenders. Their behaviour is much more complex and the root of their difficulties is not easy to find. These students need you to be fair, firm and most importantly, consistent. Your first attempt has to be to get to know these students on a different level. You have to know and be aware of what is happening in their heads and in their world.

Many of your students do not live the safe life you live. Some come to school with nothing to eat. Some have been awake all night listening to domestic violence. Some had no parents at home the night before.

The issues they deal with often affect their ability to stay focused. There is very little we can do to help their home situations but we can provide a safe place for them to spend the day. Being aware of your difficult students situations and being compassionate of their background is the first step to understanding them.

Other repeat offenders act out because of their lack of understanding of what to do or how to do it. Many of these students have had behaviour problems for years. This means that they have obvious gaps in their learning. When other students were grasping the needed skills to move forward, these students were distracted from learning. To expect them to learn like others is very stressful and often they return to the one thing they are good at getting in trouble.

These students need to know that you understand them and that you are there to help them improve their learning. They also need to know that you care enough to make them feel a part of the class. That also means that you expect them to follow the same routines and rules as everyone else. You will be surprised at the progress you can make with students when they know you care about them as people.

In their world, they need a significant other, a person they can count on, look up to and see as a model. You can be all of these simply by letting them know you understand and that you want them to be in your class. Never underestimate the power of caring.

When In Doubt, Do Nothing

> I had a summer job working for a power tool company. My job was to put jigsaw castings on a line to be painted. When the painting was complete, I took them off the line and carefully put them in a bin. Those castings that had blemishes, I threw into a recycle bin so they could be stripped and repainted. Our students are not like this. They can't be repainted after being stripped of the imperfection.

I have always told my student teachers that if a situation arises and they don't know what to do, then do nothing. I need to explain this more. What this means is that it is better to wait in some situations and get guidance from other people than to react and do something out of ignorance. We never get a second chance to fix a mistake we make with a student. Doing nothing about a situation doesn't mean you are not going to respond. Once you have spoken to your administration, colleagues or other professional, you are better prepared to deal with the situation in a positive manner. You are now prepared to deal with this student, privately and effectively.

Many times it is better to wait. It gives you time to be proactive instead of reactive and it also gives the student time to calm down. Unless this is a behaviour issue that is out of your control or is serious enough to involve others, then you have the time to deal with it correctly.

Changing Behaviour

Before you can try to change a student's behaviour, you must first correctly identify the nature of the action. The identification must be based on specific characteristics. Identifying what the student does and says is vital because it allows you to proceed through the process of changing unacceptable behaviour to acceptable behaviour. By doing this, you are pinpointing the specifics of the behaviour and avoiding generalization. You are better prepared to zero in on the exact behaviour you want to change.

Understanding the effects of the behaviour is another critical part of identifying the type of behaviour you want to address. It is important to note how the behaviour affects you, the teacher, the student and the other students in the room. By doing this you will be able to design a better solution to bring a positive and constructive change.

Most inappropriate actions are a desire, by the students, to meet a specific need they feel is preventing them from behaving as expected. The primary causes of the action may be a need for power, revenge, attention or a self-confidence. There may be additional needs such as hunger, thirst, lack of rest, escape from stress or sexuality issues. There are many factors that need to be considered when a student acts out. Take the time to identify exactly what is going on. Once you have a deep understanding of the issue, you are better prepared to come forward with a plan for change. You are also better prepared to discuss your plan with other professionals, as well as the student.

Changing and replacing behaviour does not happen quickly.

There is a belief by some that to eliminate and replace a behaviour can take up to 21 days or more. I explored this theory several years ago while working as a classroom teacher. Our French teacher was experiencing difficulty with my group of students. They were often off task and refused to listen as he spoke. Together we came up with a plan of action. Having just read this 21 day theory, I was keen to play it out. Eliminating the off-task behaviour, in class, was easily accomplished in 7 days. We consistently addressed the talking and off-task behaviour and within the first week, all students had a good understanding of what we did not want to see. They knew exactly what behaviour was unacceptable. Replacing the behaviour with appropriate performance was much more difficult. We found that if we wanted to see a new behaviour, we had to model and consistently reinforce compliance daily. Failure on our part to do this often resulted in the students falling back into their "bad habits." Once our goals had been met, we again realised the importance of reinforcing the students on a regular basis. Although new behaviour can replace old behaviour, the past is not forgotten.

If you want something to change, you must be prepared to work hard to get it and to maintain it.

Buying Behaviour

There are many programs on the market to assist you with behaviour management. The better programs are the ones that have mastered the art of common sense. I firmly believe that any program that is designed to improve student behaviour is only valuable if it is self-eliminating and cost-efficient. Once the behaviour has changed then there should be no need to continue to use the "pay off" for compliance. I have watched teachers spend countless amounts of money buying gifts for students to behave. I have seen the candies placed on their desks and the promise of free activities if everyone earns the time. These all remind me of the behavioural modification techniques used by Pavlov when he was training his dogs to comply. Students are not rats that run around a maze for the reward at the end. They should not be taught to work for a reward. The reward system could work in the short term but may create a need for higher rewards, to maintain established behaviour, in the long run. Students need to see the value of learning and the need to be responsible for their education. They need to be intrinsically motivated to behave. I maintain that by presenting an enriched, realistic and student-centred program, we can manage student behaviour by getting them actively involved and engaged in their learning. A student who is engaged sees the value of learning and knows that poor behaviour prevents them from the success they want to obtain. Students should be intrinsically motivated to behave. Engagement in learning is a major factor in classroom management.

Chapter Five
Teaching For Success / Motivating Students Through Engagement

As teachers, we should want our students to be successful. We must also believe that all students can learn. Being aware of how a student learns is critical as we guide the learner up the educational mountain. It should be obvious to everyone that not all students learn at the same pace, nor do they learn in the same way. What is a motivation to some is not to others.

Remediation for one student will not always work for another. These are very simple and basic principles—however, it is shocking how many teachers attempt to paint all students with the same brush.

Our goal as educators should be to assist, guide and coach a student as they work their way through the learning process. We need to be able to identify their progress and assess the next step required to meet continued success. We need to give students the chance to get it right, but we must also give them the strength to see their errors and learn from them. A teacher must provide ongoing feedback and a chance to redo work. If the work is not up to the standard, no mark should be final if a student is willing to improve.

Learning Styles, Multiple Intelligences and Decision-Making Styles

Understanding how students learn is as important as teaching them the skills they need to become independent learners. It is important to give them the opportunity to learn about themselves, to understand their strengths and weaknesses as learners. This information can be invaluable to you when setting up groupings. There are many types of tests available today that help students gain an understanding of their learning and personality styles.

During the first week of school, my students explored their learning styles. They were provided opportunities to test and evaluate the ways they learn. How they learn is important to their success and equally important to you as their teacher. Auditory learners can listen to you all day long, but those that are visual will tune you out very quickly unless you can support what you are saying with something they can see. Students who are tactile learners may listen for a while and may be able to see what you are talking about but unless they can play with it and get their hands on it their learning is limited. Many students use a blend of these styles. The way you teach must have a combination of methods so all students will benefit.

Understanding who they are and how they best learn helps the student understand where they fit into their learning.

As a classroom teacher I tried to select appropriate assessments that would help the students establish a beginning understanding of themselves as active participants in the learning process. Using these tests as an informal assessment tool was my way of creating a baseline observation or beginning point for the students. By no means should these tests be seen as prescriptive or finite. The intent was never to box the students into a category but rather to help them understand the complexity of their learning styles.

The Myers-Briggs Type Indicator assessment is a questionnaire designed to measure psychological preferences in how people perceive the world and how they make decisions. This test assumes that individuals are born with, or develop, certain preferred ways of thinking and acting. The test sorts some of these differences into four opposite pairs, or dichotomies. None of these types are better or worse; however, Briggs and Myers theorized that individuals prefer one overall combination of type difference.

http://www.myersbriggs.org/my mbti personality type/mbti basics/

DISC is a behavioural model that measures the behaviour of individuals in their environment or within specific situations. DISC looks at behavioural styles and preferences. The tests classify four aspects of behaviour by testing the students preferences in word association. The results fall into four defined areas:

Dominance - relating to assertiveness and control

Influence - relating to social situations and communication

Steadiness - relating to patience and persistence

Conscientiousness - relating to organization

http://www.teamapproach.com/discprofile.asp

Learning Styles are various approaches or ways of learning. They involve methods, particular to a student, that allow that individual to learn best. One of the most common and widely used categories of the various types of learning styles is Fleming's VARK model. These learning styles are divided into four specific areas:

1. Visual Learners

2. Auditory Learners

3. Reading/Writing-Preference Learners

4. Kinesthetic Learners or Tactile Learners

Fleming believes that visual learners have a preference for seeing (think in pictures, visual aids such as overhead slides, diagrams, smart boards, models, etc.). Auditory learners best learn through listening (lectures, discussions, cds, podcasts etc.). Tactile/kinesthetic learners prefer to learn via experience—moving, touching, and doing (active exploration of the world; science projects, experiments, etc.)

http://www.vark learn.com/english/index.asp

The theory of Multiple Intelligences was developed by Dr. Howard Gardner in 1983. Dr. Gardner, Professor of Cognition and Education at Harvard University Graduate School of Education, suggests there are eight (possibly more) different intelligences to account for a broader range of human potential in children and adults. These different intelligences can be directly related to student learning and to how the student shows understanding of a concept. These intelligences are:

Linguistic Intelligence (word smart)

Logical/Mathematical (number/reasoning smart)

Spatial Intelligence (picture smart)

Bodily/Kinesthetic Intelligence (body smart)

Interpersonal Intelligence (people smart)

Intrapersonal Intelligence (self smart)

Naturalist Intelligence (nature smart)

Existential Intelligence (conceptual smart)

http://www.thomasarmstrong.com/multiple_intelligences.htm

How students make decisions is not only critical to their learning but also an important consideration when setting up group assignments. Most students have a blend or combination of these decision-making styles. Some students are very strong in the generation of ideas but often find it difficult to move beyond their ideas to complete the assignment. Other students are people-oriented and will do anything to promote harmony in the group. These students are usually peacemakers and serve an important role in the team; however, like the ideas people, completing the task at hand can be difficult. Students who concentrate on the process have a great understanding of what needs to be done. They don't always share a sense of group and often lack the ideas to get the assignment completed. The product style of decision making offers the student an excellent understanding of what the finished assignment will look like; however, without the ideas, the group harmony and a good understanding of what is required the finished product often lacks the depth required. Most students share a gentle blend of these skills. Being aware of how they work in a group and how they approach assignments is very important for them and you to understand. Huge gaps and areas of weakness need to be addressed throughout the year and opportunities should be provided to help the student improve in all areas of decision making.

I wanted my students to explore their decision-making style involving collaboration with a group activity. Using a collaboration profile questionnaire I borrowed from a course I took one summer, students were asked to identify their strengths when working in a small group situation. Students evaluated themselves on how they worked on a particular task. Some students were very strong when it came to generating ideas, others found their strength in working with others and creating harmony within a group. Some students found that they were very good at understanding the process involved in completing an assignment, while others could clearly see the end product. Most students have a blend of all of these, however, usually one area dominated.

These collaboration styles were first discussed by Ichak Adizes in his book "Mastering Change, The Power of Mutual Trust and Respect in Personal Life, Family Life, Business and Society" (1991). The creators of the Leading Edge, a company that provides seminars and training to Human Service professionals such as counsellors, therapists, social workers, educators, and health care professionals, took these styles and divided them into four categories:

Ideas - these people are full of ideas and creative solutions

People - these team members strive to create harmony within the group

Process - these people understand the steps involved to reaching the goal

Product - these team members have a great understanding of how the finished product should look

Although the categories are based on an informal profile and not intended to be used as a psychometric measure, it is interesting to see how students view themselves in a group situation.

Upon completion of the activity, I did a Four Corner exercise where I had all students meet with others of similar styles. The Ideas, People, Process and Product people all shared their discoveries and were asked to complete an assignment where they would explain more about their style to the rest of the class. To my surprise, none of the groups were successful. The Idea people had tons of great ideas but couldn't move beyond the idea. The People students had a great time, laughing and talking about the whole experience but failed to move beyond the social event. The Process students knew exactly what steps were required to complete the assignment but could not move forward because of their lack of ideas and inability to get along.

The Product group knew what they wanted the end product to look like but could not get to it because they were lacking ideas, structure and coordination. Knowing how students learn will help you successfully fill the groups that you have set up. Not only do we want our students to have the opportunity to discuss and share in the class setup we have established, we also want to provide them with every opportunity to be successful in these groups. Groups must be set up for success. They cannot be randomly established. It is important to create productive groups where all students feel supported and valued. This is also a concept to understand when working with other staff members. It is important to be aware of the skills and collaboration styles of each member of the team.

Differentiation of instruction and assessment are important for all students. If we agree that students have different combinations of learning styles, multiple intelligences and decision-making styles, then it makes perfect sense that we must address these differences when we present students with new ideas and skills. To ask the entire class to turn to page 47 in the text and answer questions 1-10 serves very little purpose. Few students learn this way. I am aware that many teachers see this as a proven method of successful teaching. I tend to disagree. The way you present your information has to be as varied as the students you have in your class, Their individual needs have to be considered if you expect all students to learn. You have to find a way to make this new material connect with your students, connect with their prior learning and with how it will relate to their world.

Years ago, I had a student in my grade eight class who struggled with written language. Years of frustration had left him with a defeated attitude. He could not see himself as a learner due large to his inability to show his understanding in writing. I came to realize that he was very articulate when he spoke about things he knew. I asked him to make oral presentations to the class as a way to show his understanding of the topics we were exploring and I helped him plan and organize. His confidence grew quickly and soon he began to see himself in a different light.

Several years passed and I ran into him one night when I was playing in a local club. I asked how he was and what he was doing. I was overwhelmed when he told me he was in teacher's college and preparing to be a high school history teacher. He told me that his confidence grew stronger after he left me and that he started to believe in himself as a learner. The more he believed in himself the easier it was for him to meet his challenges and overcome his years of frustrations. I still beam with pride today as I reflect back on this experience.

Differentiation of Instruction

Brain research has confirmed what experienced teachers have known for years. No two students are alike in the way they learn.

What works for one student will not necessarily work for another. Differentiation of instruction involves creating multiple paths that accommodate the individual's learning needs, abilities and interests. By doing this, the students become more involved in their own learning. Differentiation can occur in many different ways involving curriculum content, the process, the final product and the learning environment.

Historically, differentiation was used when working with LD students in a withdrawal setting or with gifted students. Recently, the concept of differentiated instruction has been applied to all students across the learning continuum. The use of technology has also become an essential tool when providing students with unique learning experiences and opportunities.

Content is the knowledge, skills and attitudes we want our students to learn. Research indicates that prior to our instruction, one third of our class will already have a full understanding of what will be taught, one third will have little to no understanding and the remaining students are at the stage of developing understanding. If we begin a new concept with an activity that evaluates student's prior knowledge, we may be able to "compact" student learning for some of the students. Compacting is used for students who have a good understanding of the concept prior to your teaching. Students who clearly demonstrate a grasp of the skills and concepts are given the opportunity to apply their knowledge by working ahead or independently on assignments and related projects. These students will be accelerating their learning, while others are working at developing a beginning understanding at a slower or decelerated pace.

When I was very young my parents put my sister and me into piano lessons. We had a music teacher who lived across the road and every Friday night, my sister and I would wander over for our lessons. My teacher, for some reason, felt that it was important to keep both of us at the same stage of our piano-playing development. My sister and I had much different talents, when it came to music. My sister saw practice as a dreadful experience, where I, on the other hand, loved playing the piano. Even though I was very competent at playing a particular song, my teacher would have me repeat the material the next week if my sister had struggled with her lessons. I wanted to move forward because I already knew what I had to do. I became very frustrated when I was prevented from moving forward at a quicker pace. The same applies to the students in our classrooms. It must be very frustrating for our students, who have many acquired skills and concepts to sit and endure our lessons, when they already know the topic. They need the freedom to move forward and to use their knowledge of these concepts and make personal connections in other areas of the curriculum.

Process can be defined as the steps we use when the students explore and develop an understanding of a concept. Differentiation of process involves varying learning activities, using alternative ways for students to manipulate the ideas being presented, and providing varied and creative methods for the students to record their understanding. The use of technology, graphic organizers, mind maps, concept maps, charts and diagrams can effectively facilitate differing levels of cognitive processing in all students, regardless of their learning abilities. Advanced students may work on activities with higher level thinking and increased complexity.

A product is what students use to demonstrate their mastery of a skill or concept. Not all students can effectively show their understanding in the same way. Often, the product we require our students to use provides a very limited opportunity for them to show their full understanding.

The students need to be provided with a choice of how they will show understanding. Students who are working below grade level may need to show a modified understanding of the concept in a way that is unique to them. Students who have quickly grasped the skills will be motivated when given a variety of choices. The goal is for our students to demonstrate understanding. We must be creative when we give them the opportunity to show this understanding.

The way curriculum is being presented in our classrooms today is significantly different from the way it has been traditionally presented. The learning environment has changed significantly. No longer is a teacher seen as the "sage on the stage" or the "face in the space." Our knowledge of how students learn has become more complex and as a result teachers are developing strategies to meet the unique needs of the learner. Students' individual talents, learning styles, multiple intelligences and social development have given teachers a better understanding of the learner and as a result planning has become complex and child centered. The role of the teacher is changing from instructor to coach. We provide students with the skills they need to grasp a concept by using a variety of teaching strategies. We analyse their individual progress and provide them with next step opportunities. We ask critical questions to help them develop a deeper and more meaningful understanding and provide challenges for them to make connections to their inner learning and prior knowledge. The way we evaluate is more specific and based on assessment for learning, rather than assessment of learning. Assessment will addressed in detail later.

The more we understand about the learner, the more we must change our learning environment to address these specific needs.

Strategies for Differentiation

Compacting the Curriculum - means modifying or streamlining the curriculum to allow a student to move at a quicker pace, thus providing time for the student to pursue an alternative topic or to explore the topic in greater depth. This form of differentiation is used with students who display advanced knowledge of the material. These students usually complete assignments quickly and with great accuracy. They demonstrate that they are capable of working independently.

Adjusting Questions - all students are answering important questions that require them to think but the questions are targeted towards the students' ability and readiness levels. Written "tests" may have students assigned specific questions based on their learning needs, but make sure all students are presented with challenging opportunities.

Tiered Assignments - a series of related tasks of varying complexity, relating to essential understanding and key skills. Assignments are designed with alternative ways of reaching the same goal based on individual student needs.

Acceleration / Deceleration - adjusting the pace of the curriculum. Some students move through the material at a quicker pace, while others need a slower approach in order to experience success.

Flexible Groupings - allows a student to be appropriately challenged by providing movement between ability groups. A student may show strength in one area and weakness in another. The use of flexible grouping provides the student the opportunity to benefit from working with others of similar ability, while preventing labelling.

Peer Teaching - gives a student the opportunity to reinforce his or her understanding of a topic. By being an "expert," the student can gain invaluable practice by being given the chance to re-teach a concept to peers.

Graphic Organizers - allows a student to display understanding of a concept in a way that is consistent with his or her learning style. The use of charts, mind maps, flowcharts and so on gives the student an opportunity to see the concept in a different way.

Independent Study Projects - provides students with the opportunity to explore a topic of specific interest to them. The degree of help and structure required for the students is dependent on their ability to plan, manage information and use time effectively.

Buddy-Studies - allows two or three students to work on the same project. Students share the research, analyze and organize. Students collaborate for understanding, however, each is responsible for their own project. Students are evaluated independently for their own planning, time management and accomplishment.

Project-Based Learning - is an approach to teaching in which students, working in collaborative groups, explore real world problems and challenges as they develop cross-curricular skills.

Differentiated Instruction and Technology

Thirty years ago, when I first began teaching, there was very little technology in our classrooms. An overhead projector, film strip viewer and a 16 millimetre movie projector were about all the teacher had to work with. The use of technology to reinforce learning was virtually unheard of and seldom fit into the teaching methods of that time. The textbook was the only true source of instruction. Over my thirty-year career in teaching, technology has become more and more relevant to the learning process. The use of computer programs to remediate student understanding has become a common place in our school system. We use the computer in a variety of ways to help our students learn and to become more involved in their learning.

The students we work with today are much different than those of thirty years ago. Today, the students grow up with technology as a critical part of their lives. They are tech-savvy before they even come to school. It has also been argued that these students are hardwired differently than we are and, therefore, learn differently because of the technological explosion. Regardless, we must be aware of the world these students are living in. Information is easily attainable, fast and constantly changing. The way students communicate with each other is instantaneous. They learn from webcasts, text messages, emails.... in ways that are often foreign to us. Teachers and school boards have a tendency of shying away from the things they don't fully understand. It is not uncommon for a teacher to prohibit the use of technologies they can't control. Although this may be seen as necessary by some, it is preventing the students from showing their knowledge in a way that they best understand. Often we ask students to demonstrate understanding with methods that are extremely old and long outdated.

To increase student engagement we need to tap into their world.

They need to be taught how to use their technology in a positive and effective way. They need to be given the choice of showing their knowledge and growth in ways that are comfortable to them.

Differentiation, through the use of technology, is beneficial in many ways. When used effectively, students can be engaged in learning experiences which provide authentic and challenging tasks that involve real world problems and situations. They can work in a global community where they can explore, develop, and test a hypothesis using scientific models and virtual manipulatives. Students can explore topics of specific interest to them and present their understanding in unique and creative ways. The students can develop high-level thinking, clear and concise communication skills.

The value of using technology, when presenting the content or the skills and attitudes, becomes apparent when we allow the students to explore these concepts at a level that meets their needs as learners. Some students will be exposed to the concept at a basic level, while others will gain a deeper and more complex understanding. All students are exploring the concept, the only difference is the depth and speed at which they go.

The process or stages through which the students progress, as they develop an understanding of the topic, can be specifically tailored to the learning styles of the students. The needs of the visual, auditory and kinesthetic learners can all be met by employing technology in the classroom. Through careful teaching, the students can become self-directed learners using the inquiry process. We are allowing the students to "play" with the concept and to discover and uncover the concepts being explored. Technology offers the students a variety of methods to record and organize their understanding. The use of graphic organizers, tables, charts, spreadsheets, power points, etc. provides real and meaningful engagement with the concept.

The ways that our students display their understanding of a concept can be greatly enhanced through the use of technology. The more opportunity students have to use technology, the better they will understand the advantages of each program. The goal for the learner is to select a program or a method that will best illustrate their understanding of a topic. There are many ways a student can show understanding. The use of multimedia, text with graphics, book trailers, slide shows, movie making, digital and analog recording, power points, digital story telling and graphic organizers are just a few of the many tools available to students.

Other examples include:

Word Art - mini-books, stationary, tables and charts, reports, business cards, business letters, post cards, signs, webpages, photos, clip art, drawing tools, flow charts, original art

Power Point - presentations, animations, timelines, illustrated stories, posters, e-portfolios

Movie Maker - film production, booktrailers, tableaux

Excel - posters, banners, graphs, charts, stock market, data base, budgets, timelines,

Publishing - newspapers, magazines, brochures, calendars, booklets, fliers, posters

Inspiration/Kidspiration - webs, graphic organizers, timelines

Smartboards - presentations, manipulatives,

The use of technology involves much more than sitting a group of students in front of a computer. It cannot be used as a fancy notebook nor should it be seen as a place to fill in time. Technology skills must be taught to the students and used to enhance their learning. The students need to see the computer as a learning tool. The teacher must see it as an important part of the learning process. Be sure that the tasks are of an appropriate cognitive level. Don't be taken in by gimmicks. Low-level learning is still low-level learning even if done on a computer. Asking key questions and using critical thinking must be part of every learning experience.

Student Engagement

Asking a student to be interested in a topic of your choice is no easy task. You must find a way to make your teaching real, meaningful and relevant.

The more personal connections a student attaches to the topic, the more the student will become engaged in the learning process.

The older the student becomes, the more frequently you will

be asked why they are doing this. It is very important that you establish the real world connection at the outset. Make them see the need to buy in because it is a concept or skill with relevance to them and their future learning.

The more a student feels they have a choice and a voice in their learning, the easier it is for them to accept their involvement.

Giving students ownership of their learning is another key component in student engagement. Through differentiation, you can provide the learners with a variety of ways for them to acquire an understanding of the topic or skill and also give them options of how they will demonstrate their knowledge. Remember we all learn differently. We also need to show our understanding in a way that is unique to us. Some students can show knowledge through the writing process. They are capable of demonstrating their understanding in an articulate, sequential format through the use of written language. Other students find this very difficult and get frustrated when this format is the only option available to them. They may know the concept as well as other students but cannot demonstrate their knowledge effectively in writing. These students need an outlet, a way of showing what they know. They need a way to feel valued as learners. As the teacher and learning coach, you need to be aware of these needs and give all students the option to demonstrate understanding.

Understanding a concept or skill is only one part of the learning process. A student also needs to have this knowledge reinforced in their own minds. The knowledge needs to be firmly in place for future connections. There is a saying that says "If you really want to know something then teach it." This idea is important in student engagement. If we want students to internalize a topic we must give them an audience to work with. When students share their understanding with others, they tend to personalize what they know and it becomes more real for them.

By explaining and sharing understanding, the student gains a greater awareness of the topic and will retain the learning for a longer period of time.

There are many benefits to providing a student with an audience. Students are aware that when they are presenting to their peer group, they are being "judged" by someone other than their teachers. Often you will see a student work and rework their assignment to get it just right. One student that comes to mind is a young man who had a gift for oral communication. Using an integrated curriculum approach, students were often given the opportunity to explore topics of interest to them, providing the content of their research fit the theme being explored. This student had a deep interest in World War One and never missed an opportunity to make a presentation on the topic. Seldom could he keep his presentations under one hour. As articulate as he was, he had a severe problem with spelling. His power point presentations were well organized and engaging—however, spelling impaired the quality of his work. When he returned to school in the fall, he was excited about presenting as he felt he had gained new knowledge and was eager to find an audience. He presented several times throughout the year. Each presentation was stronger than the one before. Something very special had happened. All of his presentations were perfect with regard to his spelling. I asked him what had happened and why his assignments were spelling error free. He told me he knew that the students respected him for his knowledge but he felt his spelling errors prevented them from understanding the depth of his knowledge. He knew that he had to improve his spelling if they were to take him seriously. Nothing can replace an internal drive to improve. Students need to have a reason to work hard and working for their own self-improvement is a powerful motivator.

A student must feel safe in their learning environment. To be successful risk takers, they need to know that you will be there if they fall.

They need to know that they can trust you and lastly, they need to feel that you trust them. Trust is a two-way street.

Your trust and their trust builds upon each other. New teachers often get lost in this area. They either have blind trust in their students or want to control them to the point that there is no trust at all. I see trust as something that is earned and cannot be demanded.

Designing successful experiences for the student is an important stage of building trust. A large part of teaching should go into the careful planning of your lessons. You need to build in the opportunity for all students to feel success in the experience you provide. The door must be open for all. Students need to know in their mind that if they put forth a good effort, they will succeed. Nothing builds success like success.

Power of Thinking Outside the Box

I have always enjoyed watching the behaviours of the younger students in the schools I have taught in. My heart always filled with joy as I watched them skip and dance down the hall. They were filled with energy, excitement and wonder. As they got older they tended to lose that enthusiasm and the skip was replaced with a slow saunter. I have asked myself his question, "When and why do they lose the skip in their walk?" After years of reflection, I have come to the conclusion that there are many contributing factors, of which we have little control, such as peer pressure and family situations. There is, however, one factor we have great control over, that being the way we teach.

What we teach and how we teach has a significant impact on

the development of self-esteem, self-confidence, engagement and attitude. We are partially to blame for the loss of that vital skip in a student's walk. The school system "educates" the joy out of learning.

Sir Ken Robinson, chair of the UK Government's report on creativity, education and the economy, suggests that young people lose their ability to think in "divergent or non-linear ways," a key component of creativity, throughout their early years in school. Divergent thinking is a thought process or method which helps students generate ideas. It is critical for the development of creative thinking and problem solving skills. Of 1,600 children aged 3 to 5 who were tested, 98% showed they could think in divergent ways. By the time they were aged 8 to 10, 32% could think divergently. When the same test was applied to 13 to 15-year-olds, only 10% could think in this way. And when the test was used with 200,000 25-year-olds, only 2% could think divergently. Education is driven by the idea of one answer and divergent thinking becomes stifled. Robinson claims that creativity is the 'genetic code' of education and said it was essential for the new economic circumstances of the 21st century. (United Kingdom Literacy Trust, November 6, 2005)

Traditionally, the education system has placed a huge emphasis on the development of literacy and numeracy skills. Academic success is measured by our achievements in these specific areas. Those of us who struggled with reading, writing and arithmetic often viewed ourselves as academic failures, despite our success beyond formal education. The need to grasp the main concepts has often been at the expense of divergent thinking skills.

Many of our students who are "buying out" of education or underachieving are doing so based on their internal beliefs that they are failures.

With such a heavy emphasis in these two specific areas on content acquisition, we are missing the opportunity to allow students to find their creative strengths and talents and meet success in other areas of the curriculum. That is not to say that these two areas are not important. They are critical in the development of the learner. What is important to understand is that there is more to learning than literacy and numeracy. Divergent thinking and creativity need to be developed in all areas of the curriculum, including reading, writing and mathematics.

Our role as teachers must be to help students develop and maintain their creative thinking skills. We must provide them the opportunity to be creative and to think outside the box in all areas of the curriculum. By doing so, student motivation and engagement will improve, self-esteem and self-confidence will grow, overall performance will increase and ultimately higher standards in education will be achieved. We may even be able to put the skip back into many students' walk.

Creativity is thought of, by some teachers, as something "extra" we do with students. It is often believed that creativity is a skill reserved for a few gifted students or for those with talents in specific areas. All students have creative capacity, combined with special talents and strengths. Creativity can be applied throughout the curriculum. It is an invaluable skill that lies waiting to be discovered in each of our students.

The advantage of developing strong creative thinking skills in our students is that it will help them solve problems but will also help them find problems we didn't know exist. Students need to sense and find potential problems for themselves as well as finding solutions. Students need more opportunities to generate ideas, to look at the world in a different way, to play with different possibilities and alternative solutions.

There are many methods and strategies that can be used to foster creative thinking in our students. Each has specific techniques for generating ideas with individuals or groups. The students need to be able to make connections beyond their traditional way of looking at the world.

Edward de Bono promotes lateral thinking through the application of the "Six Thinking Hats" method. "Six Thinking Hats" is a powerful technique that helps students look at important decisions from a number of different perspectives and points of view. Students are encouraged to look at a situation from a position that may not agree with the way they traditionally see things. As such, it helps the students understand the full complexity of a decision, and discover issues, opportunities and problems which they may never have thought about

The use of PMI (Plus, Minus and Interesting) is another strategy used by de Bono to help students see the other side of an issue. For years, I used the PMI strategies as a start to each day. The moment the students entered my class in the morning, they were to begin to work on the PMI question on the front board. This helped "kick start" their engagement as well as give me time to attend to my administrative duties such as attendance, collecting money for pizza or field trips and so on.

Another strategy that can be used to develop creative thinking skills was developed by Gordon and Prince. Their method asks students to make "synectic" connection. Through this process, students make the strange familiar and the familiar strange. Synectic thinking is the process of discovering the links that unite seemingly disconnected elements through the use of analogies and metaphors. It is a way of mentally taking things apart and putting them together to create new insight for all types of problems.

Mind maps have been used for centuries in education and can be used for a variety of purposes. The modern use of mind mapping was developed by Tony Buzon as a way of creating and organizing thought through the use of a diagram. Words, ideas and other tasks are linked around a central key word or theme. Mind maps help students generate, visualize, structure and classify ideas and can be used for problem solving, decision making, organizing and studying. I have used mind maps as a way of having the students record their understanding of a specific topic or concept. These mind maps were used as a study tool and even used as a reference on some tests. The greatest success came when I used mind maps in oral testing. I would allow the students to use their diagram as a guide for their discussions. I was impressed with the deep understanding students showed. The mind map "unlocked" a sea of knowledge and understanding and allowed them to make visual connections and links.

Assessment of Creativity

It only makes sense that we should be "creative" when we assess a student's creativity. You cannot successfully measure a student's growth by simply administering a final test.

It is not the final product alone that is important here, although a culminating task may be formally assessed at the end of the unit. Creativity is a long and slow process that involves many stages. The use of diagnostic and formative evaluation should be used throughout the creative experience. Teachers can draw on many forms of evidence such as children's attitudes, participation in class, portfolios, conference and group discussions, organizing charts and so on.

Chapter Six
Make it Real, Make it Relevant, Make it Personal

The main focus of this chapter is to show how student engagement can be taken to a deep level. What I am about to share with you is a teaching method that has evolved over many years of teaching. It began with the integration of real world experiences into the curriculum. What I found was that when students could relate what they were learning to the world around them, the more they became engaged.

I was in my third year of teaching when I was struck by a "lighting bolt" that changed the way I taught for the rest of my career. I was teaching a lesson on grammar. Like all teachers at that time I was standing at the front of the class lecturing them on the parts of speech. I had carefully written several sentences on the board and we were in the process of underlining the subject with a single line, the predicate with a double line, round brackets around the adjectives, square brackets around the adverbs and so on. As I turn to the class for a volunteer to come forward I looked deeply into the eyes of my students. They were all sitting there totally unmotivated, uninterested, seemingly void of engagement. I was shocked at what I was seeing and I thought to myself, "What the hell am I doing?" I knew in my heart there had to be a better way to engage students. I had to find a way to get them interested and excited about learning. The rest of my career was dedicated to finding ways to provide a challenging and exciting program for my students.

After many years of working with such strategies as cooperative learning, Bloom's Taxonomy, curriculum integration, differentiation, project-based learning and backward design, I developed a program that brought together my understanding of how students become engaged in the learning process. The success of the program and the engagement of the students went far beyond my expectations.

To successfully teach using this approach, you must be competent in many areas. A deep understanding of the curriculum is critical. Classroom management skills must be firmly developed and a strong understanding of how students learn as individuals is very important. Flexibility and creativity are required on an ongoing basis and you must possess a deep understanding of assessment and evaluation.

What I would suggest is that as a new teacher you start slowly and begin with something you know you can accomplish. Try using cooperative learning strategies in your program. Always be on the lookout for real world examples to show the students. Design your lessons with opportunities for students to use divergent thinking. Give them the opportunity to develop questions about a topic. Use Bloom's Taxonomy as a guide for the questions you are asking.

Students need to know how to take their understanding of a topic to levels beyond knowledge and application. Spend time in the beginning of the year having the students understand Bloom's Taxonomy. This allows them to explore a topic in ways beyond the surface. They ask themselves and others deeper questions that ultimately increase the depth of their understanding. Give students ownership of their own learning and make them want to do well for themselves.

Nothing fosters learning more than an internal passion for a topic. Once the fire has been lit and the engagement begins, there is no stopping the imagination nor the depth of understanding.

It has never been our job, as teachers, to fill a child's mind with information.

Our ultimate goal should be to light the fire in each child's soul and to create an endless thirst for truth.

Our students come to us daily, hearts filled with hopes and dreams. We must do our very best to give them the opportunities they need to meet their goals. We need to give them ownership of their learning and the chance to meet success in ways that are unique to them. As described by Ben Zander, the great conductor, teacher and writer, we must put the shine in our student's eyes. If we don't see that shine, then we must ask ourselves what it is that we are doing wrong. Nothing speaks louder than the sparkle in a young person's eyes. If we see it we know we have touched their souls.

Several years ago I was given the opportunity to build a program that would take students to new heights of engagement. I was teaching grades 7 and 8 in a small inner city school in Eastern Ontario. The student population contained its share of at-risk students and the school was recognized as being "high needs" by our Board of Education. In partnership with a colleague and under the careful guidance of our administrator, we set off to discover the art of engaging students. First, we explored existing programs in other jurisdictions that were designed to foster advanced learning through experiential education. We immediately saw the benefits of such an approach for our learners' needs. We noticed the reactions of the students to this approach and were amazed at the sense of ownership each of them shared. We agreed that to truly engage our students in their learning process, we had to create a program that was meaningful, reality-based and which catered to the specific needs and learning styles of our student population. It was at this point that the process of creating the "Current Experience" began. It became the most rewarding experience of my thirty years of teaching. Never had I worked harder and never had I seen such positive results in students. The energy that was created in our program was so much more than I had ever imagined and I strongly believe that there is no better way to teach. We had struck the mother lode and our students were rich beyond their dreams.

The first step is to select an appropriate topic for an integrated project-based unit. This is critical to the success of an authentic learning environment. The topics must be real, relevant to students' lives, controversial and capable of being integrated into many areas of the curriculum. The selected topic must provide the teacher the opportunity to cover the essential learning and enduring understandings in the curriculum. We have explored such topics as the Environment, Halifax Explosion, Social Injustice, Global Warming, and Media and Technology. Each of these units were of great interest to our students and created the environment where curiosity and critical thinking could take place.

Selecting a topic that is real for the students is important.

All students want to know that what they learn has something to do with the world beyond school. Often these topics are current and information is easily attainable. We want the students to be able to explore a vast amount of information giving them a knowledge base. It is also important that this information is available in a variety of formats, text, video, etc. The wider the information sources, the deeper the engagement for all students. Students need to be given the opportunity to become engaged regardless of their learning strengths.

Often what we think will be of interest to our students is not what they find exciting. The more relevant a topic is to the world of the student, the more a student will become engaged. The world in which they live in is very fast paced and filled with constant change. Information is at their fingertips and they want answers to questions now. They don't like to wait.

Controversy is their world and many students are masters at arguing. Playing the devil's advocate comes naturally to them.

Selecting a topic that has a variety of opinions and views can be very exciting for the students.

They see the opportunity to express their opinions openly. Controversy opens the door to many learning experiences. Opinion writing, debates, trials, simulation, role playing and discussions are only a few of the possibilities. Engagement increases when opinions can be shared with a real audience.

Once a topic has been selected, it is important to bring the topic home. The relevancy of what is being explored must be felt locally, in the student's own community.

For this reason, each unit is driven by one essential question. Everything that is discovered by the student is reflected back to the essential question. Since our school community is located on the St. Lawrence Seaway, in the case of this year's Environmental unit, we asked how the St. Lawrence Seaway would be affected by global warming. We want the students to see that climate change affects everyone, including them. When setting up the Halifax Explosion unit, we asked if our city could handle a disaster of this nature. Again, we want the students to look at their community in terms of the topic. The more we can connect a student to the topic the greater the chance for engagement and eventually a passion.

The first stage of learning around a topic begins with the collection of data and information. As their learning coach, we need to guide students through this process. Our students each have different skill levels when gathering and assessing information. We must diagnose their level of competency and spend extra time with those requiring our assistance. The internet has become their first and sometimes only source of information. As a result, we need to give the students the skills to evaluate the validity of the information presented to them. The students must formally assess the sites they are using as a resource and measure the value of the information gathered against suitable criteria. The students need to be given the appropriate skills to become critical thinkers. To effectively answer the essential question, the students must learn to suspend judgement until all of the facts are weighed in. Only then are they forming valid and justified opinions. For this reason the essential question is reviewed throughout the unit and addressed formally at the end.

Students must have opportunities to seek information from other sources such as video, magazine articles, by interviewing guest speakers or through personal experience. During the global warming unit, students were exposed to many sources of information such as film, newspaper and magazine articles, and guest speakers from the Frontenac Arch Biosphere and Environment Canada. Some proposed that they attend a Global Symposium on Climate Change. It is important to stay open to possibilities and to take the learning in the direction of the learner. The more information we expose the student to, the deeper the knowledge base and the more a student will become engaged.

Understanding increases dramatically when we can integrate the selected topic and essential question into other areas of our curriculum.

The Environment unit involved examining data management and statistics from a variety of sources. The students used real numbers and data to explore the severity of climate change. They were given the opportunity to calculate their ecological footprints and compare their results with others. Ecosystems were explored in depth and a trip to a local stream reinforced the importance of our water systems. They met professionals in our community that work with the environment and were given firsthand experiences involving stream preservation. They wrote opinion pieces and letters to our Members of Parliament asking important environmental questions. The significance of the St. Lawrence Seaway was explored through a historical and economic context. As the integration increases, so too does understanding. The students got the opportunity to see how all of this fits together. Rather than thinking in separate disciplines, they think in connections.

The development of critical thinking skills is crucial for student understanding. We must find ways to ask the students important questions that will help them further explore the topic and develop a deeper understanding of the issues involved. We need to provide them with the skills and opportunities to think independently, thus allowing them to evaluate and clarify their values. Critical thinking allows them to develop a personal perspective and draw conclusions based on fair mindedness while avoiding oversimplifications and bias.

During the Global Warming and Environmental units, the students were asked to evaluate the statistics and data from different points of view. Often we would put them in situations that made them argue a topic from a position that was opposite from their own personally held view.

As the students began to develop some expertise on the topic, we gave them the opportunity to explore areas of special interest that have came to light through their independent research. Students were asked to explore this personal area of interest and to make a formal presentation to the class at the conclusion of the unit. We did this in the form of a symposium. Again, the essential question must remain central to the topic. The specific format of the presentations were determined in consultation with us. The students were aware of their multiple intelligence and had countless opportunities throughout the term to explore a variety of presentation formats such as Power Point, Inspiration, dramatic presentations, models, artistic displays, song writing, podcasts and so on. Each presentation had a minimum 15-minute time limit and a mandatory oral component. All students were responsible for creating their own evaluation rubric, which was used to evaluate their presentations. The skills for making presentations were formally taught to the class with several examples from previous years being used as exemplars. When the students saw how it was done in the past, they were often eager to surpass the standards.

Independent research is invaluable for many reasons. An opportunity must be provided for students to explore a topic from a personal interest point of view. They need the freedom to develop a passion for the topic in an area of interest to them.

The more personalized the topic becomes, the better the chances are for engagement and ultimately a passion for learning.

When students get a chance to share their knowledge with others, their understanding increases dramatically. Giving the students an audience gives them a reason for learning. Sharing their opinions gives them a chance to clarify their understanding. If you want them to know something, then give them a chance to teach it.

Returning to the essential question at the end of the unit gives the student the chance to reflect on all they have gathered. They use their knowledge and experiences to bring the topic to a conclusion. It helps them finalize their opinion and validate their understanding.

The passion for learning starts with the teacher. Throughout this entire process, the teacher is the key component. Our interest and enthusiasm is contagious and our desire to learn must serve as a model for our students.

The students must believe that what they are studying is of importance to all of us. They need to tap into our energy and our excitement. We need to be there to ask the important questions.

We need to guide them to make inferences, predictions and interpretations. We need to give them the courage and opportunities to develop the skills to be effective learners. We must give them an audience with whom to share their knowledge and we must truly care about what they say. We must recognize the role technology plays in their lives and give them the skills to use this technology to their advantage.

The more we tie into their world, the better the engagement, the deeper the understanding and the better the chance for the development of a passion for learning and for staying in school longer.

Chapter Seven
Assessment and Evaluation / Report Card Writing

An effective teacher has a thorough understanding of evaluation and assessment and is fully aware of how each is a measuring tool for student growth and program modification. Grading a student is much more complex than simply marking a piece of work and handing it back to the student. There must be a careful balance between assessment **for learning,** which helps identify the next step in student learning, and assessment **of learning,** which is used for the evaluation of what has been learned. Although the two may appear as different forms of assessment, with different goals, they are not necessarily unrelated as formative assessment should lead up to successful completion of a summative task.

When we assess our student's performance we are looking at where they are at this moment in time and making suggestions for their next step in the learning process as well as our next step in the delivery of program.

Not all students will get to the top of the educational mountain at the same time. Not all students learn at the same pace. They can, however, all make great strides towards the top of the mountain if we evaluate them for learning rather than of learning. The difference being that we are not always looking at where they are as the final destination but rather as a step towards mastering specific skills. Our mission, as effective evaluators, is to guide students to move beyond the stage they are presently performing at.

This we do by analysing their progress, through our use of assessment, and wisely deciding what is needed to be done next.

There are two forms of evaluation, formative and summative. Formative evaluation, which is always part of the instructional process, involves a variety of observations through such structures as general observation, conferencing, mini-quizzes, questioning, student and peer evaluation, journals, presentations, small group discussions and so on. The key to this form of evaluation is the direct involvement of the student in the process. Adjustments are made by both the student and the teacher in the learning process. The student is made aware of where he or she is in the mastery of the skill and is involved in the design of the next steps required. Data that we collect at this stage should not be used in the formulation of a final grade. This data is used to guide us and the learner.

Summative evaluation is a method used to find out how much a student knows at a specific point in time. This is "show time." Because of the accountability nature of summative evaluation, this is often the measure used as part of the grading process. Summative evaluation usually involves a form of an end of unit "test." Both types of evaluation are very important. Each, however, is designed for a specific purpose. You must have a deep understanding of both forms of assessment to be effective as a classroom teacher.

Students need the chance to get it right. Assessment must be ongoing and viewed as progressive. A student who is struggling with a concept should be given the opportunity to go back and rework the assignment. A grade or a mark does not have to be final. It should be open to change as the student grasps the learning. It is not how quickly he or she gets up the mountain that is important. It is each step along the way that carries the most significance. The opportunity for improvement must be provided to each student if we are going to see them progress as

successful learners. They need to be able to fail, correct the situation and then move forward. Our ongoing feedback is critical to this process.

> When I turned fifty-three I decided I wanted to ride a motorcycle. I had never learned to ride when I was younger so I signed up for a course at a local community college. During our first class we were given the course outline and expectations and told that on the last day we would be tested individually. Success in the program was based completely on that final test. If we passed the test, we were given our license. If we failed then we were required to do the course again. This is what summative evaluation is all about. We were being evaluated on our skills at the completion of the program.
>
> During the next two days, we were taken through a series of skills development. Each skill was broken down to its basic elements. We were given time to practice each skill and we were being carefully monitored as we rehearsed. The instructors observed everything we did and when it was apparent that we were struggling with a specific skill, they would take us aside individually, to help us move forward in the development of that area of weakness. We were all fully aware when we were struggling with a skill and required assistance to meet success in that area before we could move on to the next skill. This is an example of formative assessment. My instructors were not making a final decision on my ability to drive a motorcycle during this part of the course. They were assessing my skills at each stage through observation. They would modify their instruction and I would adjust my learning through the effective use of formative assessment. My inability to perform certain skills during the learning process had no influence on the final grade given at the end of the course; however, through the use of formative assessment my skills were strengthened and

chance for meeting success were greatly improved. Their assessment at each stage was only used as a guide for them and myself. The final evaluation was based on the driving test. Could I safely drive the motorcycle or not? The final test was based on a scoring rubric, leaving little room for flexibility. The test score was final. No time was given for second chances or practice. The ongoing formative assessment helped me become successful and pass the test.

Balanced assessment is critical if learning is to take place. We must be able to collect data that will show us what our students are learning. We need to know that what we are doing is effective.

It is our responsibility to constantly monitor student growth and the quality of our teaching methods. Evaluation is for us as much as it is for our students.

It is easy to place blame on the students for poor performance in the mastery of skills and concepts. The hard truth is that we must look at ourselves closely when this happens. We have an equal and shared responsibility for the learning that takes place in our classrooms. We must ask ourselves what we, as instructors and learning coaches, need to do to foster learning in our students.

Knowledge of the Curriculum

Knowledge of the curriculum you are teaching is critical for all teachers. You must be fully aware of what you are required to teach. You need to know what specific skills and essential understandings you are addressing at all times. This can only be accomplished through studying the curriculum documents and speaking with more experienced teachers. Once you have a handle on what you are required to teach, it is imperative that you prepare a detailed long-range plan of how you will present the curriculum to your students. The long-range plan will become a blueprint for you to use as you move forward in the delivery of your program. Like all plans, changes and modifications will be made as you progress throughout the year. An effective long-range plan should be established in connection with the way you intend to use both formative and summative evaluation. What you are teaching, and ultimately reporting on, must be connected to the curriculum you will be covering each term. When you set up your mark book to match the specific skills you are teaching, you will find the process of writing your report cards much easier. You will be commenting on exactly what you have measured. Your formative evaluation will help you establish comments regarding the process, whereas the summative evaluation will give you the final grades for each term.

This process becomes more difficult when using an integrated approach. When you blend essential understandings across subject areas, you must be aware of exactly what skills you are focussing on. It is much like working with a jigsaw puzzle. All of the parts of the curriculum will fit into the puzzle. Your job is to know exactly which skill goes where. It is very important to establish a detailed marking system which will allow the flexibility for this style of teaching. Unfortunately, report cards are not designed for this way of teaching. You must dissect the integrated skills and place them into separate categories. Hopefully, someday, we will begin to see report cards that will make this effective style of teaching more user-friendly when it comes to evaluation and assessment.

How do you come up with a report card mark in each subject area? You must have the data before you can begin the process of creating a mark.

The days are long gone when we add up the marks, divide by the number of marks and create an average.

This process was an inappropriate way of conducting business. Not everything we evaluate carries the same weight, nor is everything we assess part of summative evaluation. Therefore, it is important that your formal evaluation measures exactly what you have taught.

Remember that not all students learn the same way and it is also true that not all students can show their understanding in the same way. Just as we modify our teaching style to meet the needs of the learner, we must also modify our evaluation methods to meet their specific needs.

Once we have created an effective summative evaluation process, then we must look at the grades we have accumulated for a consistent mark. It is important that we look for this consistency. This way we are getting a true picture of a student's performance. A bad day for a student should not necessarily have a huge impact on a student's mark if all other marks fall in a different range. At times, we will find ourselves torn between moving a mark in a certain direction. This is where formative evaluation can be used as a guide in which direction we will tip the scale. Caution needs to be used here—remember, formative evaluation is not used to generate a grade. However, if used carefully, it can be used to help you with a decision regarding the establishment of a final mark.

You must be prepared to justify your grades at any time. Your principal may ask how you came up with a mark, the students need to be aware of their progress and I can guarantee you that at some point a parent will ask you. Keep your records thorough and up to date. Make anecdotal comments to support your evaluation. Nothing is more professional than a well-kept marking system that matches your long-range plans.

Report card comments have changed drastically throughout the years. We have moved from writing a single comment about the student as a learner, to addressing progress in each subject area specifically. We are asked to comment on what the student can and can't do, and what are the next steps. You must find something positive to say even when things are not progressing well for a student. Comments have to be written for both students and parents, as well as educators. All report cards are placed in a student file and moved on to the next teacher. Therefore, it is important that your comments are written clearly and address specific skills. The next steps have to be attainable and offer guidance for improvement. Be careful not to use teacher language as most parents and students will not understand what you are saying. The most important thing is to be honest and accurate in a positive way. Don't write what you think the parents want to read. Honesty is so important. If a student is average but hard working, don't write a comment that makes him or her sound like a top student. Doing this makes it difficult for other teachers who will comment honestly in the years to follow. So many times we hear comments from parents that claim their child has never experienced any problems until now and this is the first time they had been told there are difficulties. A true reflection of a student's growth is so important. Be honest and be accurate.

The way report cards are created is always changing. Most report cards are now created on a computer. This has made the process a bit easier in one way but also creates a multitude of other technological problems such as glitches, loss of data and computer freezes.

Always check your report cards carefully before sending them home. The report card is a reflection of you as a professional. You cannot have your reports filled with careless mistakes. Be careful.

There are teachers who feel that being honest and grading a student accurately can be a reflection on their ability to teach. These teachers struggle with students who do not achieve well in class. They don't want the marks given to be drastically different from previous years. Occasionally, you will see them looking at prior report cards for guidance. They modify or alter marks to match the student's performance from prior years. They don't want to alarm parents with an honest evaluation. They want to be liked by the students. This is a very dangerous strategy. Parents and students are not given correct information and ultimately the next teacher is left with a huge problem to address and correct. Honesty is always the best way to approach evaluation. Only when we present the situation the way it really is can we match the next steps to help the student improve and grow. When a discrepancy occurs, it can be helpful to consult with past teachers to see why you are out of sync.

Most schools ask that the reports be submitted to the principal for reading prior to be sent home. This often eliminates careless spelling and grammar errors. Never trust the built-in spell check. I had a terrible experience one year when I used a spell check on my comments. Assuming that the computer had made the needed changes, I proceeded to hand my reports in for principal approval. What I didn't know was that the computer had changed some of the student's names. Devon became Demon, Gabby became Gassy.... can you imagine the parents reading this?

Chapter Eight
The Interview and The Parent

The report cards have been written, photocopied, folded, placed in envelopes and sent home. Interview times have been assigned and now it is time to meet the parents face to face. It is always good to have a plan on how you are going to approach this first meeting. The interview format can take many different shapes of which I will discuss in a moment; however, the main purpose of the interview is to discuss the student's progress and make the necessary suggestions for improvement next term.

Meeting the parents is very important on many levels. Most significant is the support level. You need and want the parents to be an equal partner in the learning process of their child. You want them to be on board with you. You want them to see that you care about their child and that you are providing a safe learning environment. They need to see you as organized and prepared and knowledgeable about your grade or subject. When parents are surveyed about what they see as important in school, the safety of their child is always at the top of the list. Always keep this in mind when you are dealing with parents.

In good times and in bad, the parents want their sons and daughters treated fairly and with a guarantee of personal, physical and emotional safety. They will be watching you closely to see if you are providing this.

The Interview Format

Interviews have changed over the years from teacher lead to student lead with various combinations in between. Ultimately the parent wants some time with you one on one. Regardless of how you set up the interview keep this in mind.

Teacher Lead....teacher does all the talking, student is there to be held accountable

Student Lead....student takes the lead by showing, explaining, teacher is there in a supporting role

Variations......teacher and student take equal role in the process

I wanted the student present at the interview. Since we are discussing a student's progress it is important that he or she be a part of the process. The older the students are, the more involved they can and should be. The students need to be engaged in the discussion. It is up to them to explain what they have been doing and what are the next steps required to move forward. Don't be surprised to see your student take on a different persona with their parents present. It is not unusual to see them become totally unresponsive and passive. Others become quite vocal and defensive. You never really know what you are going to see until the interview begins.

Students are used to being accountable to you and they are used to being accountable to their parents but it is a different situation when they have to be accountable to both of you at the same time. This is very stressful for some students. Be there for them. Let them know you care.

Usually before the interview, each student sits down with the parents and shows them samples of their work. This is done with a portfolio that is created at the beginning of the year and updated on a regular basis. A proper portfolio should show progress over time and evidence of learning. It should never just be a random collection of "good work."

The use of E-Portfolios can serve the same purpose. Students with direction from the teacher, create a collection of their work and evidence of their learning. This gives the parents a chance to see what their child has been doing. It is much easier to discuss progress when everyone has a reference point to work from. Students are also required to create, in advance, a summary sheet that can be used when discussing their work throughout the term. This summary sheet discusses everything from subjects and attitudes to personal reflections. The student begins the formal interview by reviewing the summary sheet. The advantage of this is that the student immediately is assuming responsibility for their learning.

Often you will see a student become very negative about themselves. It is our responsibility to step in and steer the interview in a positive direction. The interview should never be a put down. The parents need to see what has occurred during the term and what needs to be done next. Being negative does not help a student grow, nor does it show that you care about them. Be honest, be truthful, be informative, but always try to protect the student. Good teachers don't use this as an opportunity to get even.

A good interview often requires you to be a good listener. You really need to be aware of what the parent and the student are saying. Clarify anything you don't understand. Ask questions so you fully understand. Parents are often unclear about what is happening in the class. They usually get one point of view, that of their child. Situations are often distorted in the child's favour. Students often tell parents that they did not understand what was required of them. Basically, a student's lack of achievement is usually the teacher's fault because you wouldn't help them. We all know this is not true; however, you must be ready in advance as to how you will deal with this. Nothing can replace solid evidence and good documentation. Keep your mark book up to date, record behaviour concerns, record dates and times of parent calls and contacts, and have the student portfolio current.

Nothing soothes a concerned parent better than your readiness and organization. Stay calm and don't take it personally. If you handle the situation correctly and continue to show how much you care, parents will join you in finding the next step to help their child meet success.

What happens at an interview is usually predictable; however, some parents come armed with a hidden agenda. At times, parents talk with other parents about small issues that have become much larger through the Coffee Club. It is always good if you are aware of this in advance and can be prepared for how you will respond. If you have been given a warning, or if you sense an interview could be difficult, don't hesitate to involve your administration. It is always wise to keep your supervisors informed of upcoming problems. After all, a disgruntled parent is going to go to them anyway; they too need to be prepared.

There are times when you are totally unprepared for what is coming. A great interview all of a sudden explodes into something you didn't see. The old saying, "When in doubt, do nothing," also applies here. If you are unprepared for a response, explain that you will need to set another time to discuss this issue. This will allow you time to collect your thoughts, gather supporting evidence and speak to your administration. If the parent is not willing to wait, then call administration immediately. Remember, don't open your mouth and slit your throat by being unprepared.

Often during an interview you will agree to provide some information or to set a certain activity into action. Always write down what you have told the parents you will do. You will be surprised at how quickly things will leave your well-organized mind after thirty interviews. The parents will definitely check back to see if you have followed through on your plan.

Your word to a parent is only as good as your actions. You want them to trust you and to be an equal partner. You have to be true to your word. If you don't plan on doing something don't tell them you will in the first place. If during the interview you tell the parents you will contact them or do a follow up at a certain time, be sure to follow through.

The way parents behave during an interview is often varied. Some sit quietly and listen attentively to everything you have to say. Others want to dominate the conversation. Often you will sit across the table with significant others, boyfriends, stepparents, aunts, uncles, grandparents. These people are there in a supporting role for the parent. Occasionally, a student's worker from a social agency will be in attendance as a way to protect the interests of the child and the parent. Regardless of who is present, remain focused on the goal of the interview, that being the student's progress and the next steps required.

It can be very interesting to see how parents with different cultural backgrounds react in the interview. Cultures that highly respect education place a great deal of confidence in the teacher. They usually sit and listen very carefully. They want to know where their child is in relationship to other students and what they can do at home to ensure success for their daughters and sons. Academic success is very important to these parents. The more educated a parent is, the more accountable you will have to be. These parents have been to school and have some knowledge of what should be happening. These parents have researched the ministry guidelines and have been directly involved in the writing of IEP's and special programs for their child. You must be prepared to deal with these parents and their deep concerns. These parents will want to see evidence. Be prepared ahead of time. These are not the people you want to scramble in front of.

A difference can also be seen, at times, between mothers and fathers. Moms are very concerned about their child's emotional well being. This is their baby you are discussing. They want the best for their child, both socially and academically. Dads, on the other hand, are often more focused on the academic results. He wants to know how his child is doing and what is going to be done to help improve these results. Of course, this is a huge generalization. The best results in an interview occur when Mom, Dad and the child show up together with one common interest, the development of the child.

The most difficult interviews involve parents that exhibit anger towards their former spouses. When families break up, some children are held at "ransom." The parents see the interview as an opportunity to show their disgust and resentment for each other. It is very easy for these interviews to lose focus and deteriorate quickly into mud slinging. This is not something you want to be apart of. You must redirect the interview back to the student. You are not a social worker or marriage counselor; however, these situations often give you great insight into what the student is dealing outside of school. It can't be easy for them at home.

During an interview, it is not uncommon for parents to express their concerns about their child's progress in other classes. It is wise to note caution when this occurs. You have an ethical and professional responsibility to your colleagues. It is not up to you to account for what happens in another teacher's class. You are not in a position to explain or justify. When another teacher's name is brought into the interview you must immediately suggest that they meet and discuss their concerns with that teacher. This is not a discussion you need nor should you want to engage in.

Neither do you want to discuss other students during an interview. Parents will often bring up another student's name. Stay focused on their child. You have a professional responsibility and obligation to each child in your class. The progress and behaviour of other students is of no concern to these parents. Tell them straight out, you are not at liberty to engage in this discussion. They may not be happy, but you are also telling them you will not discuss their child with others. You must maintain trust with all partners.

Parents frequently want to compare your class with school when they were young. There is no similarity and to make a connection based on prior school experiences is wrong. Parents need to know that what you are doing in your classroom and with your subjects is based on sound pedagogy and proven research. The way you teach comes from experience and specialized training in education. It is your job to explain and teach the parent, you really don't need to defend yourself or your positions.

Once a parent is confident that what you are doing is based on a solid and in-depth understanding of educational strategies and good teaching practices, you will find most will back off and let you continue with you work.

Always conclude the interview by reviewing the expectations of all concerned. End the interview on a positive note. Thank everyone for coming, shake their hands and smile with confidence. You are all on the same team, working towards the same goal.

Chapter Nine
Administration

This chapter could easily be summed up in six words: "**No surprise is a good surprise.**" Always keep your administrators informed about potential problems. They do not like being blindsided. Many parents, when calling the school, ask to speak to the principal directly. Be wise and let them know what is happening before these calls arrive. This will give them the opportunity to be prepared to deal with the situation in advance.

Your administration is the most valuable resource in your school. They are the buffer between you and the parents as well as an important advocate for the students you teach. You may not always agree with the direction in which they would like the school to go, but you must find a way to work with them. Forget about the behind-closed-door criticism that many teachers enjoy engaging in. Don't get involved in the negative comments. Stay focused and see your administrators as positive members of your teaching team. They are not the enemy—they have an important job to do and carry a heavy responsibility.

During my thirty years of teaching I was very fortunate to have worked with some of the best administrators in our system. Each principal and vice principal brought with them their own unique leadership style. It is vital, as a beginning teacher, to fully understand the role of an administrator and how they set the direction of the school. Your ability to work effectively with your administration is important.

Principals have many responsibilities they must carry out within the school environment. Most important, the principal is the head of the educational setting and acts in a supervisory role. Those who work in a school are accountable to their administrator. The administrator provides guidance for teachers and students as well as being an important link to the community in general. The principal must plan and implement the daily routines for the school. The principal is also the curriculum leader in the school and is responsible for monitoring teacher performance. They ensure that students are receiving the educational requirements and activity requirements that are necessary in a balanced learning environment.

The administration in your school works under the guidance of their supervisors. Like you, they are accountable to others. Often a principal must follow the direction set out by their superiors. Like you, they are accountable to the Ministry of Education and to the implementation of Board or District goals and visions and must respond directly to the requirements of the system as set out by the Director and Superintendents. They must follow directives, board protocol and guidelines. They don't own as many of the decisions as you would like to think.

To successfully work with an administrator, it is important to understand their leadership style. Once you are aware of how they do business, then you can find ways of creating a positive working environment that will benefit you, your students, your colleagues and the parents. There are three main types of leadership styles administrators follow: the Authoritarian, the Participator and the Delegator. Most administrators are a blend of these three styles and a highly successful administrator knows when to effectively shift from one leadership style to another. Often an administrator will use a specific style to match the job that must be done. For example, when a decision must be made that affects the entire school, the Authoritarian approach may be used after all of the facts have been considered. When a decision must be made that will affect a specific group within the school, an administrator may shift into a Participator or democratic role where they will involve a small group in the decision-making process. This style allows the responsibility for the decision to be shared. Smaller decisions that do not have a huge effect on the school can often be decided using a Delegatory style, allowing those involved to make the judgement; however, the final decision must be accepted by the administrator, thus placing them back in the Authoritarian role.

Teacher Evaluation

Your administrator has a responsibility to evaluate your teaching performance. The procedure for this varies according to district and board, however, the goal of the process is always the same, to make you a better teacher. Principals are checking to see that you are doing your job as outlined by the Ministry of Education. They will observe your strengths and offer suggestions for improvement. Keep in mind that your students are always the beneficiaries of this evaluation process. Be open to feedback and not defensive. You cannot view your evaluation as a threat. Feedback, like formative assessment, helps improve your performance.

Anything that will help you improve as a teacher will always benefit your students.

The evaluation process has changed drastically over the last few years. No longer is an evaluation based solely on the basis of a classroom visit. Observed teaching is only one step in the evaluation procedure. Teacher portfolios and conferences give the classroom teacher a better opportunity to share with their administration the wonderful things they are doing in the class with the students. You should always be prepared for your evaluation. Keep your mark book and day plans up to date. Revise your portfolio to keep it current. When doing something that is exciting and different, invite others to see what you are doing. Take pictures and keep letters and notes in a file to share at an appropriate time. It is not always enough to know that you are doing great things with your students. A time comes when you must prove the quality of your performance. Be prepared in advance.

Extra-curriculars

There is so much more to teaching than what we do within the walls of our classroom. The establishment of a positive, trusting rapport with students leads us to activities in other areas of the school.

Students demonstrate different attitudes beyond our classroom. It is important that as teachers we get involved with the students in different ways. They need to know that we see them as more than just students sitting our class. We also want the students to see us as more than just a classroom teacher or subject specialist. Your principal wants to know that you are taking an active role is the school community.

The involvement in extra-curricular activities is not always an option for teachers. Often, at the beginning of the year you will find a list of "extra jobs" being passed around at a staff meeting. You are expected to sign up for something. It is important to see the value in this experience, not only for you, but for the students as well. By getting involved you are building a needed relationship with the staff, school and students. Look at this as a positive experience that is going to benefit everyone.

The most obvious way to get involved is through sports; however, not all teachers and students are athletes and many do not get involved. There are many other options, ranging from clubs to special events. Select an activity that you know you will do a good job at. The effort and energy you put into these extras will be returned to you by those you work with. Extra-curricular activities are important for all students. Finding different ways to help students become engaged in school life is important. Even those students who don't fit in need some way of being engaged.

Professional Development

Staying current with the best teaching practices available is key to any successful teacher.

Many workshops are provided throughout the school year and during the summer months. New educational philosophies and teaching strategies are being shared on a regular basis with all teachers. A good teacher will change with the times. The students I taught thirty years ago do not reflect the students I taught at the end of my career. The world has changed and so have the students I worked with. Although change can be frightening at times, it is a necessary requirement in the educational system. You cannot cling to old teaching methods. Your administrator wants to see evidence of current educational practices in your class. Always remember that the students are the ones who gain the most when you use good and proven successful teaching strategies.

Classroom management is a critical part of the evaluation process. It doesn't really matter how great your ideas are if you can't get the students to do the work. Your administrator already is aware of your classroom management skills long before they will ever evaluate your teaching performance. How you deal with behaviour issues in your class has already been observed and noted.

Say what you want in the conference—your actions in the class have already spoken louder than your words.

A principal may want to look at your mark book. They will be making several important observations when they look at what you have recorded. They want to see a variety of evaluation methods, both summative and formative. They need to see that you have conferenced with your students and made anecdotal notes. They need to know that you have given the students a variety of ways to show what they know. You may be asked to explain, in detail, how you will arrive at a report card mark using the information you have recorded. Again, be prepared in advance.

Your day book is an interactive tool for you to use that shows the direction you are heading on a daily basis. It should reflect the goals and objectives you are attempting to accomplish as well as how you plan to assess student performance. The amount of detail you write varies from teacher to teacher; however, your administrators want to see that you have a strong sense of direction and knowledge of where you are going. Many of these goals will have already been laid out in your long-range plans that are in the principal's possession; however, your daybook shows how you are accomplishing these goals on a daily basis.

Day plans are important regardless of how experienced you are as a teacher. You must keep them up to date. You will be asked to show them.

Throughout the school year, we have many conversations with students and parents. Always keep a record of these discussions. This is important, as you may need to look back on a previous conversation to refresh your memory. Your administrator may ask for evidence of these types of conversations during the evaluation process. They are invaluable.

It is always hoped that your teacher evaluation will be positive. The feedback you receive during this process should always be taken in a positive light. If you are asked to improve in an area, it is always for the benefit of you and your students. Your administrator will offer you suggestions and opportunities to improve.

They may set up a chance for you to visit and work with other teachers who are strong in your area of need. They may send you to specific workshops to improve your skills. There are usually few surprises during evaluation. You know of your strengths and needs. You see it on a daily basis and know what you need to work on. A good teacher is constantly trying to improve their craft.

On occasion an evaluation is not positive. This is usually a sign that your teaching is in need of drastic improvement. You may have been given many opportunities to improve and still you struggle. Your attitude may be interfering with your performance. The principal may decide to place you on an improvement plan, which is a formal process based on specific look fors. What this means is that you are going to be carefully observed and many opportunities will be provided to help you improve your teaching skills. Although this can be devastating, it is important to realize that your inability to successfully work in a classroom will have a serious effect on the students. As an advocate for the students, your administrator is doing what is required to ensure that learning is taking place.

At this stage of the evaluation process, you may want to contact your union or federation. They will guide you in your responsibilities and will ensure that everything is being done to help you improve. They will act as an advocate for you if you feel you have been unjustly treated, but keep in mind that they cannot help you if you do not want to improve.

Your administrator is key to the success of the school. It is so much easier to find ways to work with them. They have a huge responsibility and a very heavy workload. Keep in mind that you are all on the same team and that it is the student that you care about.

Chapter Ten
Colleagues / Team Building

There is an expression that says "It takes a whole village to raise a child." This is also true in the education of children. It takes an entire school to begin to educate a student. It is so important that all teachers work together towards this goal.

Teachers should never see themselves as responsible for just the students is their class. Education is a shared responsibility.

Working together toward a common goal is not an easy task. Not all teachers share the same vision. Teachers, like students, are all at different stages of development. Some are fully implementing "the plan," others are beginning to implement and a few don't understand completely what the goal really is. It is so important that all teachers get on board.

A well-oiled machine can achieve greatness, whereas a team mired in conflict most often grinds to a halt, with the students being the victims.

Teachers are educated, trained individuals who have experienced years of being in control of their futures and ultimately in control of the students they teach. They are used to being heard and they like to have their opinions valued and accepted. Although it is not difficult for teachers to work in a team with thirty students, it can, at times, be difficult to work in a smaller team consisting of staff members. Developing a strong working relationship with your peers is important not only to you emotionally and professionally but also important to your school and the students. Coming to school everyday should be a positive experience, something you look forward to. You should feel safe in this environment and feel accepted and valued by both students and staff.

So much can be accomplished when the staff works together. There is a positive creative energy in the building that is contagious and the students are the prime beneficiary.

Most schools are designed around divisions or subject areas. As a result, teachers tend to meet frequently in these divisions. Teachers often identify themselves according to their teams. I, for example, spent most of my career being an intermediate teacher. I planned, shared and set goals with my intermediate team members. My contact with the other divisions was minimal. I was not always aware of what they were doing nor were they aware of what was happening in our division. The term division by definition implies a divide. Although it is efficient to work as teams, I also suggest that it is equally important to work as a cohesive unit of all divisions. It is important that everyone is a part of the master plan and that all teachers share in the education of the students. Imagine the possibilities for student learning if we all share what we know about our students.

Effective teams and divisions should be able to build on the success of others. There are two types of teachers in a school. Those who, when they see others being successful, immediately become upset and concerned and want to know why "they" are getting the attention and those who see success, embrace it and want to join in, thus making themselves part of the experience. The teacher that is not interested in the successes of the school often becomes isolated from the positive experiences. Those who join in find they grow both professionally and emotionally from the energy being created.

Team Building

How do you build a successful team and still allow for individual differences? Although this may sound difficult, we do this with our students every day. We design lessons and experiences to help them become effective team members and we encourage them to be accepting of others. We teach them how to listen objectively, how to compromise, how to accept the opinions of others, how to disagree in an agreeable manner, how to take their turns, how to follow the team norms and why it is important to stay on task. The same rules apply to teachers. To be an effective team member you have to set aside your personal biases and agenda and be willing to accept the views of others. The most important goal of a successful team or division is to stay focused on the vision of the school.

Never lose sight of what you are really there for, that being the students.

Your job, as a team, is to enhance the school " vision" by creating enriched learning experiences for your students. To do this you must meet regularly to discuss your individual and team successes and failures. You will need to identify your divisional needs based on baseline testing and observations. As a team, you will review and analyse test scores and student work. You will set new goals and revise old ones. The process is ongoing and a very important part of your teaching.

Teachers need to see the team as a powerful and positive experience. The professional growth that can be achieved in teams is invaluable. The accomplishments that can be achieved far surpass the achievements of teachers as individuals. When teams are regarded as valuable, a positive environment begins to grow. When teachers see their colleagues as vital resources and contributors, a positive energy begins to grow and the possibilities are endless.

Several years ago I experienced the energy created by a team working with a single goal. The school I was working in was having a difficult time with behaviour management. Our administrators were determined to find a solution to the problem and after much research they came up with a plan. All teachers would be trained in the area of Fred Jones and his program dealing with Positive Classroom Discipline and Instruction. No one at the school had any experience in this area and therefore, everyone was on the same playing field from the beginning. The first things our administrators did was to discuss with the staff the need for change. It was important that each teacher buy into the plan. We all agreed that behaviour was our number one issue and that something needed to be done. The second thing that needed to be agreed upon was our desire for training. We all agreed and from that moment on you could feel the energy starting to rise. A few teachers were selected to be trained by Fred Jones and upon the completion of the course, they would return and train the rest of the staff. The training was the beginning and from then on all teachers were speaking the same language, sharing the same ideas, working with the same vision. The third thing our administration did was remove some of the barriers that would make it difficult for teachers to become fully engaged. The implementation of the program brought the staff and students together at a level never experienced before. The expectations were the same in each classroom. Behaviour changed almost immediately. Teachers and students could feel the difference from the first day. Staff members would meet during and after school to discuss problems and progress with the implementation. Everyone was helping each other. Professional dialogue was ongoing and positive. Those that struggled were helped by others. It was an amazing experience for everyone involved and it showed the power of a team focussing on a shared vision.

Listening for Team Effectiveness

"I remembered how he used to teach this idea in the Group Process class back at Brandeis. I had scoffed back then, thinking this was hardly a lesson plan for a university course. Learning to pay attention? How important could that be? I now know it is more important than almost everything they taught us in college."

"Tuesdays With Morrie" by Mitch Albom (1997)

One of the key factors that affects the success of a team is listening skills. Too often team members hear only what they want to hear. The information that is being presented is misinterpreted. Many people have a tendency to selectively listen, hearing only what fits into their personal vision and matches their views. For a team to become truly effective, each team member must put aside their professional bias and actively listen to the group discussion. Each group member must be prepared to alter or modify their opinions. By closing your ears to alternate points of view, you are effectively shutting down the effectiveness of the team.

Active listening is a skill that has to be learned. It should be no surprise that teachers, as well as students, are not very good at it. Good listening takes time. Perhaps that is why God gave us two ears and one mouth so that we could hear twice as much as we say. A good listener is free of preconceptions and prejudices and listens with an open mind and an open heart. They concentrate totally on the speaker and what is being said, avoiding the temptation of mentally preparing an immediate response. An effective listener, gives the speaker both visual and oral encouragement. A good listener allows the speaker to finish what they are saying and avoid interrupting as much as possible. Active listeners eliminate judgement by asking open questions that develop clarity and understanding of the speaker's intent and feelings. If they are unsure of the speakers message they ask questions for understanding. The speaker is always thanked for their contribution.

Dealing with Conflict and Criticism on the Team

Conflict happens! We see it between members of families, between friends and between nations. Conflict happens in groups, and as elsewhere, it isn't always bad. In many cases, conflict can lead to a better understanding of issues and other people, as well as creative ways to solve problems or take advantage of opportunities.

Conflicts happen in groups for many reasons. Some causes of conflict are the result of miscommunication and misunderstanding, real or perceived differences in needs and priorities, real or perceived differences in values, perceptions, beliefs and attitudes. Each of these sources of conflict can be approached with specific strategies. In general, conflicts arising from miscommunication and misinformation are easier to resolve than those arising from differences in needs and priorities. Differences in values and beliefs and those arising from how things are structured are more difficult than conflicts over information and priorities. The first step in managing and resolving conflict is to determine which of these sources are the biggest contributors to your conflict.

The basic skills for dealing with conflict have to do with describing the conflict in such a way that people don't feel personally attacked.

You can do this by asking questions to determine the sources of the conflict and offering a description, testing it to see if others also see things as you do. By continuing to question and test, the group will come to understand what the conflict is about.

In order to solve a problem in your team, the most important skill is listening—listening for facts as well as feelings.

You convey that you are listening through the language of your body (by making eye contact, by smiling, by leaning forward, by nodding) and by restating and summarizing what someone has said. This kind of acknowledgement of another person is often a powerful way to defuse situations that have become tense or disruptive. You also convey that you are listening fully by asking questions that allow speakers to open up, allowing them to focus on what they are feeling, thinking and wanting to happen.

Process for finding solutions to conflict

Time and ground rules: Find a time when people can meet just to focus on the conflict and its solution. Suggest and get group "buy-in" around ground rules such as "no personal attacks," "ask questions to understand," "one person speaks at a time" and others.

Venting: Allow each party (or those with common views) to describe the conflict in turn and discuss how they feel about it. Ask questions that elicit responses beyond yes or no: "What happened?" "How did you feel?" "What impact has the conflict had on you?" Ask clarifying questions: "Can you phrase that another way so I can understand?" "Say more about that." And open the way for others in the group to ask similar clarifying questions. Ask those not involved in the conflict to refrain from stating how they feel, but rather to ask open-ended, nonjudgmental questions so that each party feels fully heard.

Summarizing: Restate the key facts, feelings and impacts each party has shared about the conflict. Ask the parties and group members to add to your summary as needed. Then ask for any observations about the situation.

Desired outcome: Ask the parties and group members to describe what the group would be like if this conflict were resolved. What impacts would a resolution have on the group's ability to do its work and maintain relationships among members?

Seek shared interests: Ask the parties and the group if they see any shared interests among the conflicting positions.

Range of solutions: Restate the desired outcome and shared interests. Ask for all the possible solutions to this conflict.

Test for support: Try to narrow the range of solutions by asking which ones seem to best bring the desired outcomes and meet the most number of shared interests.

Test for agreement: See how willing the parties are to adopt one or a combination of the solutions. If agreement doesn't come easily, ask what would have to change to make a particular solution acceptable.

Record the agreement: Write it down for the group records, so it can be reviewed when needed.

Evaluate the agreement: Decide on a time frame for looking at how well the solution is working; evaluate and modify it as needed.

I have always found it important to summarize and record the points discussed in a meeting prior to the members leaving. So many times we exit a meeting thinking everyone is on the same page when the truth is no one has a clear understanding of what was agreed upon. I recall many planning meetings designed to establish the assignment of roles in an upcoming school activity. Once everyone had their input into the nature of what was to be done, different responsibilities would be divided among the team members. Often, a week later, there would be great confusion over who was doing what. Summarizing and recording the information makes these situations easier to deal with and greatly improves the chance of everyone being on board.

Types of Team Members

It is important to get everyone involved in the team. Group members differ in many ways. Each person has their own agenda and ways they want to participate. Knowing how each member operates can help develop a positive team experience for everyone.

Passivist: These teachers sit very quietly and offer little to nothing to the dynamics of the group. They are there because they feel obliged but beyond that will contribute nothing. These people are difficult to engage. They prefer to stay on the outside of the circle. Every attempt should be made to include these people in the decision-making process. Although they may not like to be heard, they can be very offended if left out.

Dominator: These people are very dangerous. They have an opinion and they want it to be heard. They have a tendency to monopolize the team meeting and leave very little time for others to debate or present their views. Their actions are often deliberate and their intent is to drive their ideas forward. It is necessary to set clear rules or norms in your group limiting the amount of time one individual can dominate.

Nay Sayer: It will never work! I can't do that! These group members never see the positive side of things. They know it will not work long before they try and therefore want to veto any change. These Doubting Thomases need to be presented with evidence before they will buy in. They need to be reassured that change takes place in small steps. They need to know that change won't be drastic for them.

Repeater: This group member is a very good listener. They have the ability to restate what has been discussed, making it sound like they have come up with an original idea. The fact is, the Repeater is not creative at all. They are only clarifying what has been discussed. This can be good because everyone gets a chance to hear an interpretation of the group discussion.

Pot Stirrer: These people are happiest when all group members are arguing among themselves. They will play the devil's advocate in attempt to keep everyone on edge. By doing so they are in a better position to have their ideas accepted as a way of creating harmony. You need to know their agenda and refuse to get pulled into their game.

Wedding Planner: These are the group's master planners. Everything has to be bigger than life. These people have a very difficult time working with those who don't share their grand vision. They are often find it difficult to accept other group members' opinions and become visibly upset when questioned or challenged. It is not an easy task to harness the energy of the Wedding Planner. Their goals are usually based on self needs. It is all or nothing for these people.

Mediator: The group Mediator is the person in the group who wants to create peace and harmony. They fully understand that nothing can be gained through conflict. They want everyone in the group to feel valued. The Mediator is often the assistant to the group leader. They help create the conditions required for progress to be made.

Contributor: It is hoped that all groups have positive Contributors on the team. These people are focused on the plan. They are good listeners and not only listen to other group members but also value their input. Their ideas are open to change. These group members see the team as a positive experience and recognize the potential gained by the group process. These people don't mind taking turns leading the group and enjoy sharing team responsibilities.

I Know I Know: These team members are invaluable to the group. They are confident in what they know and present their understanding with great clarity. They are often open to suggestions and see new ideas as a way to improve personal growth. They are ready and willing to share their understanding with others.

I Know I Don't Know: It can be refreshing when a team member willing acknowledges their lack of understanding. It often suggests a willingness on their part to seek new information. They are usually open to suggestions and seek understanding from those who do know. It can, however, be dangerous if this team member doesn't know because they don't want to know.

I Don't Know I Know: Some members of the team are very knowledgeable but are unaware of the depth of their understanding. Often, these teachers are doing incredible work with the students. They are current in the strategies and methods they use. These group members are invaluable because they are usually "doers." They work hard and have the best interest of the team in mind at all times.

I Don't Know I Don't Know: This is the most dangerous of all team members. They are totally unaware of their lack of understanding. In their minds they know it all. They are the first to claim they do it and they do it all the time, when in fact they do nothing. It is very difficult to communicate with these group members, as they have already formed their opinion.

There will always be disagreement in a group. This is healthy and can be very positive. There is also a danger when everyone goes with the flow. Nothing changes when people just agree to agree. The important thing is to allow everyone an appropriate amount of time to share their opinions. You need to create a safe team environment where all members feel free to share their concerns and to explore their ideas. There is nothing wrong with disagreeing in an agreeable way. Be accepting of other group members ideas and compromise if necessary. Don't lose sight of the goal of the team.

There may be times when a team gets off course and decisions are being made that you do not agree with. It could be that the team is doing something that is morally or professionally wrong. This is never the time to sit back and say nothing. If you feel that you cannot live with the direction the team is going you must speak up and, if necessary, leave the team. If the team is conspiring against your administration or another colleague, you are always wise to remove yourself from the situation. This is never something you want to be a part of. You have professional responsibilities and you must be aware of them.

There are situations that arise in schools that are just plain wrong. On the rare occasion a teacher may act inappropriately and is subject to reprimand, either legally or professionally. The "team" may feel they should rally behind the teacher for support. Please don't get involved. It is not your position to defend. Stay out of it for your own good.

School teams can become very closed and a new teacher may find it difficult to be accepted into the group. The responsibility for acceptance falls on both the shoulders of the new teacher and the shoulders of the other team members. A new teacher has to be aware that the team has been functioning effectively before he or she arrived. They have a way of conducting business and each team member has assumed a certain role in the group. You cannot expect everything to change because you are now part of the team. New teachers have to ease slowly into the team. They cannot try to dominate nor should they try to pretend they know everything. Experienced teachers are fully aware of how they felt when they first began teaching. None of us knew anything coming into teaching and gained our knowledge through experience. As a new teacher you have very little experience. Accept that and learn from others that do. The team will be very accepting of you and your ideas once you prove to them that you are committed to the team process. They will notice your contributions and you will be accepted. Take it easy and take it slow.

The experienced team members have a responsibility to make you feel welcome and to explain how decisions were made in the past. They should share with you their experience and offer assistance when required. They also have to be very open minded. They too don't know it all. Fresh and new insight is very valuable to a team. They need to recognize that as a new staff member you have positive contributions to make and that change is good for all. A new group member can add that energy required to set the team on fire. Be patient and wait for your chance, it will come.

Types of Teams

There are different types of teams in a school setting. Each team setup is designed for a specific role.

Divisional Team: These teams are made up of the teachers that instruct students in the same grade levels. They meet to discuss day-to-day business. They review instructional goals, set division standards, plan events, order materials and discuss the general progress the of the students and the division as a whole. It is within Divisional Teams that teachers discuss long-range plans for the team. They can also further discuss topics generated at staff meetings.

Professional Learning Community: PLC teams are different than a divisional team even though the members are the same. The purpose of this team is to generate professional growth. These meetings are set to discuss teaching style, techniques and strategies. PLC sessions plan to assess student growth. Plans and goals are established based on the analysis of the data. These meetings are very intense and in depth. The goal is to improve student learning by analysing and evaluating student progress and making the required adjustments.

Leadership Teams: These teams usually consist of divisional leaders, learning resource coaches and administration. The goal of this team is to share ideas and to offer input. Through this group all teachers become aware of what is happening in other divisions. It is a chance for administration to get feedback from each division and to review the vision of the school. These meetings can be very effective, as each team has an equal input in the decision-making process.

School Planning Teams: School Planning Teams are similar to Leadership Teams in that all divisions are usually represented. The main difference concerns the topics being discussed. These meetings are usually called by the administration and plans for the school are discussed.

Mentor Teams: These teams are much smaller and usually involve a teacher and their mentor. A mentor is that person on staff who has been assigned to help a newer teacher fit into the school environment. They often meet when a need arises and support or guidance is offered.

Being a mentor is a wonderful experience. There are many ways of taking on this role. Often it is something that just happens out of admiration and respect. A younger teacher eager to learn is drawn to the confidence and experience of a more senior teacher. Together they work in a partnership of sharing. The working relationship I had with one teacher over my last few years had to be described as the best experience of my entire career. He was young and keen on learning. Together we would explore new ways of teaching. We would give feedback to each other. We would discuss learning on a daily basis. I might have been the older and more experienced teacher but

I can assure you that I learned as much from him as he did from me.

In some situations a mentor is assigned by administration to help a new teacher "fit in" to the school. Those involved are usually asked to assume their role as mentor and to take on the responsibility of being there for another teacher.

Late in my career I was asked to be a mentor for a new teacher in our school. It was not something I really wanted to do as I was very busy with my new program. Instead of saying I would not have the time for this role, I took the job without comment. In hindsight, I should have spoken up. I did very little to assist the new teacher. I found myself avoiding contact with her and provided little help. There were many times when I noticed her doing things that could have been done differently. Instead of stepping forward, I ignored what was being done. I failed miserably in my role as a mentor. I let her down and, more importantly, I let myself down. I knew better and did nothing about it. I wish I had that experience back; I would do everything much better.

Working in teams can be a very positive experience for all teachers. Working with others with shared goals helps us grow as professionals and gives us the opportunity to expand our teaching abilities. Great things can be accomplished when teams work effectively. A group must recognize the power that can be gained through collaboration and cooperation.

Chapter Eleven
Your Legacy / Life Long Impact / Crisis Intervention

It is strange how an unplanned event can change our lives. Several years ago I was attending a workshop on Cooperative Learning. It was an extremely snowy day and as a result the presenter was trapped in Toronto and unable to make it to the meeting. The organizers of the workshop were caught unprepared. All of us in attendance were out of our schools with paid supply teachers back in our places. After a quick scramble, they came up with a fill-in activity. We were asked to reflect on what we wanted our legacy to be after we retire. I have never forgotten his reflective activity and what I learned about myself I carried with me for the rest of my career.

While doing workshops with student teachers I often ask them to reflect on how they want to be remembered after they retire. I ask them to write it down. Wouldn't it be wonderful if they could keep those papers and be able to look back after thirty years to see how they did?

In the last few years leading up to my retirement I found myself reflecting on my career. I had taught in several schools and had met with much success. I found myself reading notes, letters and cards I had received over the years from parents and students. I would always feel so proud of the kind words they had written.

It was a great feeling to know that during my career I had such a positive impact on so many students. They would write about how I had always been there for them and that I showed caring for them everyday. They wrote about my being there during difficult times and they talked about their excitement with the program I offered. I was fulfilling the legacy I wanted for myself.

When I was leaving teacher's college I was asked by a hiring principal what my philosophy of education was. I laughed at the time because I really didn't know how to answer that. All I did know was that I wanted to make a difference in one child's life. I knew that if I could do that then I would be a success as a person and as a teacher. I knew that the only way to successfully work with a student was to "build" them from the inside out. They had to feel good about who they were on the inside before I could put any "educational paint" on the outside, otherwise the outer coating would blister and peel away. Everything I did as a teacher was based on that simple philosophy. It never changed and never will.

Over the years you will find yourself teaching many students. You will struggle to recall their names, although you will never forget who they were and how they were as students. They will grow up on you and before long they will become parents. They always remember and they never forget how you treated them. I have run into many students throughout my career that would come up to me and say "Do you remember when?" Some of the events I can recall vividly while others have slipped my memory. I am always amazed at what memories the students hang on to.

For many years I played keyboard in a rock band. During that time I would run into many of my former students. They would come up to me and introduce themselves and we would engage in a wonderful conversation of days gone by. I was so proud of their accomplishments, regardless of what they became, after all, I was still their teacher and they treated me that way. On one occasion, I met a former student I had taught fifteen years prior.

He told me I was his favourite teacher. I beamed with pride and I asked him what I had done to deserve such an honour. I was amazed by his response. He told me that when I was teaching him his family was going through a separation and he was having a very difficult time dealing with this. He talked about how kind I was to him and how I always took the time to talk to him about how he was feeling. The conversation that stuck in his head was the time we talked about his mother's new stereo. I had long since forgotten about all of this but I can assure you that this twenty-eight year old had not. This was his memory of me. This was my legacy.

A few years ago, while playing in a club, I was told that one of my former students was in the crowd. I had taught this young lady in the third year of my teaching . She had changed so much in her appearance. When I taught her she was thirteen and now she was thirty-eight. During a break, I went over and sat with her. She told me how successful she had been in her life. I was very proud of her. Then she said something that I will never forget. She told me that I had hurt her more than any teacher she had ever had. I was dumbfounded. I wasn't expecting this. I asked her what I had done. She told me that being new to my school and in her grade eight year, she felt very uncomfortable and out of place. Being an outsider and in grade eight can be challenging for many students. The students have their cliques and the peer group is firmly established. Being a new teacher, I was doing an introduction activity so we could all get to know each other. I asked the students to write their favourite foods on a paper so I could read it out to the class and they could identify who wrote what. She told me that most of the students had written cool foods such as pizza and she had not. When I came to her name I read out her food which was" potatoes." She told me I laughed and the rest of the class laughed as well. She was embarrassed and devastated. I was totally unaware of how she was feeling at that time.

I was crushed as she told me this and I apologized. I was not aware of what I had done. I tell you this story because it reinforced for me the power of being a teacher and the importance of our legacy. After reading this you may think it was just a small thing but it was a memory that this young woman had carried with her for over twenty-five years.

Everything we do is important and everything we do is seen and remembered.

This was a very humbling experience for me, one I will never forget. What we do with students and to students is lasting. Our legacy is often defined by our actions and can be defined by one moment in time.

During my career of thirty years I have taught all kinds of students. Some have gone on to successful careers as lawyers, doctors and accountants. Some have even become teachers. There are also those who have failed in life. Some found themselves on the wrong side of the legal system and had to pay severe consequences. Regardless of where their lives have taken them they will always remember you for how you treated them as people. Recently I was entering the bank when I was stopped by a young man who asked me if I remembered him. He told me his name and we chatted for a while. He told me he was back at school but had experienced many years of hardship, including time in jail. He continued to tell me that he was a better person now and that his future was filled with hope. I said my goodbyes and upon leaving the bank he was still there. He said he wanted to tell me how good it was to see me again. As I got in my car and drove out of the parking lot I glanced back and he was still standing there waiting to see if I would look back. I did and I waved. He smiled and waved back.

As a teacher we carry such responsibility. We are respected by those we work with and they will always look to us for guidance and approval, long after they have grown up. You can never underestimate the power of caring.

Crisis Intervention

What I am about to share with you is something I hope none of you ever have to experience. I prayed that I would be able to complete my entire career without dealing with the loss of one of my students. It was something I knew I was not prepared for. It is something none of us can ever be prepared for.

Our students spend the better part of two hundred days with us. We get to know them very well. They are like our family and we come to love them as individuals. We know what excites them and what brings them to tears. We know how to set them up for success and we fill them with hopes and dreams for a future. They know that when they are with us we keep them safe and protected. We are their model of behaviour and we are who they often turn to in difficult times. At the conclusion of the day we usually stand at the door and say our good-byes followed by "We will see you tomorrow." Never can we imagine that a tragedy could be just steps beyond the school yard.

It was a cold winter day and we had just finished working on an activity that involved the students designing their new apartments. One of my students and I had just shared a few laughs over the rental costs of her apartment. She had miscalculated and was paying significantly more than her share of the rent. I was sitting with her as the bell rang. She smiled, thanked me for my help and waved as she left the class. She had only been with us for a few months. She was a very likeable student and was kind and considerate to her peers. She was so easy to work with.

Within a few minutes the air surrounding the school was filled with sirens and flashing lights. Our worst nightmare had occurred. Two of our students, my students, were hit by a train. I can still see my Educational Assistant coming through the doors of the school from the accident. She looked at me and whispered that they were ours. My life changed at that moment. The school was filled with a flurry of activities over the next few minutes. There were police officers, school board officials, students and parents. We were called to the staffroom where we were told, by the police, that one of the students was killed and the other student was in serious condition.

I left the meeting and went upstairs to my class and I sat at my desk. I just sat and looked at both student's desks. I was trying to make sense of what had just happened. My teaching colleague and best friend came in and asked me what I was going to do. Through my tears all I could say was that I didn't know. I was not prepared for this. I knew that there was school tomorrow and I knew the students would need me more than ever. I knew I had to be strong and I had to do the right thing. I just didn't know what the right thing would be.

While sitting alone in the classroom, my eyes were drawn to the desk my student had been sitting in at the end of the school day. I could immediately feel the emptiness and loss. I sat down at her desk and pulled out the last notebook she was writing in. I wanted to "feel" what she was experiencing in the last few minutes of school. What caught my attention were the doodles that were drawn on several pages. They were a reflection of her as a person. Small pictures of happy faces and animals. I could feel the tears flow as my eyes moved from drawing to drawing. I thought to myself of the many times I had asked students not to draw in their notebooks. From that moment on I never once commented on "doodles" in a student's notebook. To me they were symbols of life, something to be cherished.

I went home and was joined by other teachers. We chatted and tried to comfort each other. The same question came up again and again. What are you going to do? Shortly after that there was a knock on the door and it was one of our community police officers that was involved with our school. He told me that I had to go to the hospital as the young lady who had survived the accident was demanding to see her teacher. On the way to the hospital, the police officer told me that she was in a great deal of pain but it was important to her that I come to the hospital. Seeing her lying there in pain almost brought me to tears. I touched her arm and kissed her forehead. She thanked me for coming and said she just needed to have me there. I tell you all of this because I need you to know how important we are in a child's life. We are there for them every day. We show them in everything that we do that we care.

They need us more than they sometimes show.

I woke up the next morning after very little sleep, still unsure of what I was going to do. I knew that there would be a great deal of support at the school from various agencies. The Emergency Response Team was prepared to assist in anything that had to be done. I knew in my heart that despite all of the help available, this was a situation that I alone had to deal with. My students needed me, not strangers, at this point. I asked all of those involved if they would let me be alone with my students. I knew help was close by if I needed them.

The bell rang and the students filed in. They were holding each other. There were tears. There was anger. There were many questions. I went from student to student holding them and showing them that I was there for them. They all sat in their seats and I spoke. I could feel their eyes upon me as they held on to my every word. I talked about the accident and I asked them to reflect on the many good things they could think of about her. I asked them to think of the other student. They sat in complete silence for ten minutes. It was the longest ten minutes of my life. No one moved, no one spoke. The tension in the air was strangling. I didn't know what to do so I did nothing. I gave them time. After a few minutes, I went from desk to desk to get the discussion going. Before long, the silence was broken and we were sharing. People were talking and healing began. Support workers came in to the class soon after this and helped the students talk out there feelings.

Downstairs was a different situation. Our principal was trying to deal with the press. There were television and radio stations, newspaper reporters. Everyone wanted a story. It was important that our students be protected from the frenzy of the press. We did our best; however, the media can be persistent and interviews were conducted off school property. It was important to us that we kept everything in its proper perspective. This was a tragic situation and we didn't need it made worse by the news agencies. As teachers we have to put our full trust in our administration and their superiors. My job was in the classroom. There role was to deal with everything else.

We made it through the day and thankfully the weekend followed. I knew I had one more challenge before me as I was asked by the family to speak at the funeral. Again I knew that my students would be hanging onto my every word and they would be looking to me for strength.

The funeral was very difficult on all of us, especially when the surviving student was in attendance. The community was so supportive and helped greatly with the healing process. What I didn't know was that it was not over. My students would take a long time to move beyond this experience. There would be little situations that would trigger an emotional outbreak in the class. Tears were always close to the surface and emotions were even closer. We were all in this together and we had to be there for each other. Healing is a group process and you as the teacher must lead by example. I remember my colleague saying to me that he didn't know if he could have handled it as well as I did. My response was and still is, at times like this we must step up to the plate. It is our responsibility and obligation to our students.

We do what we have to do. I know he could have and would have done the same. Whatever it takes, we must do it.

There are many crisis situations that a teacher must be there for. The important thing to remember is that we are there in a supporting role. We have our limitations. I attended a Youth At Risk Conference in Toronto several years ago. The presentation that has remained in my mind was the one given by a renowned psychiatrist. He spoke of educators and how much he respected our profession. He commented on how he didn't feel he could do our jobs because he didn't have the knowledge. He continued to tell us that we could not do his job either because we were not trained in that area. The key point here is to know what you can do and call for help when it is beyond your expertise. We are teachers, not councillors. We can do more damage when we try to intervene in areas beyond our training.

During my thirty years of teaching, I encountered many crisis situations. Family break-ups, parent suicide, drug over-doses, domestic violence were just some of the realities my students encountered. School must be a safe haven for our students. We need to be there for them. We must keep them protected and safe. They are only children and we are the adults.

It is important that we create a level of trust with our students. There are many situations they share with us when they are looking for guidance. You must always keep in mind that we have a professional and ethical responsibility to pass certain information on. Many students will ask you to not tell their parents. This is not something we can promise. The parents need to know when their child is in danger or at-risk. Social agencies must be informed about certain situations. As a teacher you have a moral and legal responsibility to inform appropriate authorities of at-risk situations. Your first step is always to talk to your administration. They must be included as they are ultimately responsible for everything that happens in the school. Children Aid Society (CAS) and similar agencies that work with families and children often require by law that they be informed directly when serious situations arise. Be aware of your legal responsibilities.

It is very important that you inform your students that you will be there to help them in a difficult situation. It is also equally important that you tell them up front that you may have to share this information with others. The trust you are creating is based on your desire to help them get the assistance they require. Remember your role is to be supportive. There are many crisis situations beyond your control and expertise. You can make a situation much more difficult when you do not pass the problem on to a trained professional. As a teacher you must know and respect your limitations. Be there but know when to share.

Chapter Twelve
Teacher Mobility / Transfers / Retirement

During my thirty years of teaching, I taught in several schools and I had many different educational experiences. The decision to expand my educational challenges was often my choice. I felt it necessary for me professionally to move forward. Many teachers are content to work in one school and prefer to work in the same division. I don't see this as a healthy experience. The challenge for all teachers is to stay fresh and current. You must grow as a professional and grab every opportunity to expand your learning. I can't see how this is possible when you lock yourself into one learning environment. Throughout my career I was constantly revising my teaching skills. The biggest challenge for me was to take my program to another school, with different needs, to see if I could maintain the same level of teaching performance. I always viewed this as a great learning experience.

Throughout my career, I worked in primary, junior and intermediate divisions. I worked in a special education self-contained unit as well as being a special education resource teacher. I left the classroom for three years to work as a consultant for intermediate teachers in my county. These varied experiences helped me professionally and gave me a better insight into student learning. It gave me a sound understanding of the developmental progress of students at all levels and helped me to better identify the specific needs of my students.

The disadvantages of remaining in one school and one

division are obvious. You have a tendency of having a restricted view of education. Your experiences are limited to the students you teach and to the subjects you are trained in. You tend to see the school system in terms of your building. This prevents you from seeing the bigger picture. The system itself is composed of many different learning environments. You are only experiencing one small part of the whole. If you are planning on moving upward in education or if administration is your goal, it is in your best interest to get a broader view of the school system by moving to different divisions and schools.

The advantages of remaining in one place are also obvious. You know your school well and you are in tune with the school environment. You have a chance to establish your legacy and the opportunity to teach generations of students. Your impact can be long term and you have the chance to share your experience with others. You can become a consistent factor despite the constant change that takes place in all schools.

Mobility in the educational system can take place in a variety of ways. The first occurs through the transfer process or application for new teaching positions, the second involves upward mobility through role changes and the third involves forced movement by administration. The first two methods of mobility are very positive in nature, the last method can be very stressful and is often connected to teaching difficulties. Your educational woes are seldom cured through a force transfer. There is usually a deeper issue at stake.

Teaching positions become available throughout the school year. They are usually posted on your board's information site. The job is described and a deadline for application is given. The process you must follow is clearly defined by your board of education in conjunction with your union or federation. Everyone is expected to follow the process. If you are planning to move about, it will be in your best interest to become educated in the process of application. The process can change from contract to contract.

Human resources will review the applications and forward the results to the administration of that school. The administrative team will create a short list and set up an interview schedule for the successful applicants. If you have been selected, you will be called and a time will be given to you. A formal interview may be conducted. That would be at the discretion of the administration.

Other forms of transfer also take place at specific times of the year. This usually involves your local union or federation. You may be asked in advance to express your desire for a transfer and you may be asked to suggest where you would like to go and what you would like to teach. If there are available positions you could be transferred directly to that position, avoiding the application and interviewing process. Become educated with how all of this takes place at your specific school board or district.

Another type of mobility in the education system involves a change in teaching position beyond the school you are presently teaching in. It could be a request for a different assignment such as a learning resource coach or it could be a move to a position that involves added responsibilities. You may want to get more experience working with a specific type of student or a special grade. This type of movement is a much more complex change and requires detailed preparation. You are asking to be considered for a new position based on your prior performance. You will need to have your resume and portfolio up to date. Your references will have to be contacted. You will be required to become engaged in a process that can be long and detailed. If you are looking at this type of movement I would suggest that you become involved in many educational experience within and outside of your school. Volunteer your time on committees. Get out there and be seen. Be positive and show your value as a team member. At the same time you are doing this, document your experiences as you go and keep your file current. You never know when opportunity will knock and you want to be prepared.

Teacher mobility is a good thing. Change is always an opportunity to explore different avenues and experiences. Our educational system is in a constant state of change. The world around
us is moving quickly and the need to be flexible is more evident
today than at any time in the past. I would encourage all
teachers to explore different teaching opportunities both inside
and out of their school. Change is today's constant. It is here to
stay. Embrace the challenge and enjoy the ride.

Know When To Leave

Teaching is a wonderful profession. There is no other job I
can think of where you have such a deep opportunity to direct the
future. The influence we have and the impact we can make on
others is immeasurable. The significant role we play in a child's
life is so important. You cannot take this career lightly.

I always cringe every time I hear someone tell me that they
got into teaching because it is easy or because it has great holidays.
Teaching is not an easy profession. It is a complex job that blends
strategies, skills and in-depth knowledge. It is knowing how to
motivate and engage. It involves a deep understanding of how
people learn. Teaching is complex, requiring years of education
and experience to be effective. It takes dedication and commit-
ment.

I have been asked by many why I would be leaving teaching
when I am still performing at the top of my game. Why would I
leave when I still have tremendous energy and excitement for
teaching? It is because of this that I have chosen to move on. It is
because I love my profession and the children I have taught.
Everyone knows in their heart when they must pass on the torch
to newer teachers. In thirty years I have not knowingly hurt one
student I have taught. I have tried every day of my life to be there
for them. I put aside personal problems to be fully attentive to

their needs. I would be devastated if I was short-tempered or unkind to a student because I overstayed my welcome.

Many of my decisions in life have been made upon reflection of a one-time experience. A few years ago I was at a meeting in Brockville with a group of principals. One them was retiring and he was being presented with a gift from his peers. It was clear to see that he must have been highly respected by his staff and the students he worked with. I listened to his farewell speech and I internalized his message. He said he loved working with children and was proud of what he accomplished with them. He knew in his heart that he was always good to them. He was afraid that if he stayed too long he would make a mistake and unintentionally hurt one through his impatience. He knew it was time to leave. He wanted to be remember for his positive energy.

I look at my retirement as an opportunity to be remembered for the good things I accomplished. It is a chance for me to sit back and reflect on what I have learned from teaching and to share this knowledge with those who will listen. I loved teaching up to the last bell. I miss the creative excitement of working with young minds. I miss their smiling faces. I miss being there for them at times of need and I miss the opportunity of just sitting and talking to them. Children are the reason we teach. Their future is in our hands. How they see themselves is often a reflection of how hard we have worked with them. Anytime a teacher feels they are not making a positive contribution to the lives of their students, this is a time to move on, find something else to do. The wellness of our students is at risk; the potential damage is immeasurable.

The classroom teacher holds a powerful position. Once the door of our rooms close it is up to us to provide the students with a quality and rich learning experience. Any change that will occur in the teaching profession begins in the classroom.

It starts with us, our attitudes, our desire to improve, our wisdom to see and bring about results.

The requirement for new teaching strategies to meet the needs of the twenty-first century learner begins with you. We all know that we cannot continue to conduct business in the same way as when we were in school. The students sitting in our class today cannot wait for us to get direction from above. They need to be prepared for challenges and develop new skills today. It is our responsibility to take the initiative, research, learn, develop understanding and deliver.

Being a teacher for over thirty years has been a privilege and an honour. I have tried hard, on a daily basis, to be there for every student I worked with. I showed them in many ways that I cared about them as students and, most importantly, as people. I cared enough to plan lessons that would meet their individual needs as learners. I tried to be creative in the way I taught and I gave them the opportunity to explore their own creativity. I came to class every day prepared and although there were times when my personal life seemed in shambles, I left that at home. My students did not need my personal baggage. I tried to set an example by being a positive role model. I wanted them to watch me interact in a positive and fun way with my colleagues and I wanted them to see me as valuable member of my school and staff. I worked hard to stay current with new teaching practices and I was committed to improving my teaching skills.

I hope that when my students look back and reflect on me as their teacher they can all say one thing in unison: "Mr. McMillan cared, but how did he ever get that girl out of his car?"

See 1stWorld Books at:

www.1stWorldPublishing.com

See our classic collection at:

www.1stWorldLibrary.com